Praise

'*Coming Home* leverages a powerful combination of masterful coaching experience and transformative life story to give us a guide to our own deeper seeking, complemented by concrete exercises and psychology research. As Gillian McMichael peels away the deeper layers of the onion to get to her truth, I found myself doing the same. She guides us effectively to live a more empowered life on our own terms rather than remain trapped in the needs and drama of others.'

Vish Chatterji, Executive Coach and Author of *The Business Casual Yogi: Take Charge of Your Body, Mind & Career*

'Gillian believed she needed to fit in when in fact she was born to stand out. She is outstanding in her field as a transformational coach and bares her soul as she tells her deeply personal journey of self-discovery. It is inspiring, empowering and uplifting and, as you follow in her footsteps throughout her book, it may just change your life.'

Alison Ferahi, Head of Organisational Development, Scottish Ambulance Service

'I wish this book had been around when I was young and overcoming life's hurdles. It's a book that will inspire many to journey within.'

Tulsi Vagjiani, Influencer/Speaker, Pilates Rehabilitation Specialist and Reiki Grand Master

'If self-development and connecting with your true self is important to you, this book will nurture your soul. Gillian courageously opens up her emotion-filled heart to speed up people's awakening process. She shares with her readers what made it possible for her to move from feeling "not accepted" to actually being loved and recognized worldwide. You will find a real-life story full of obstacles and self-limiting beliefs to overcome, but also insights and helpful exercises that will enable you to undertake your own journey to become your best. As you read the book, you are invited to reflect on your own life. Where have you come from? Are you ready to become the architect of the life you want for yourself? Connect with your true self to become who you want to be!'

Aida Frese, MCC Global Executive Coach and Coach Supervisor, EIA, ESIA, Argentina

'I loved reading this book. Being our true selves is all too often the gift we never give. We are shaped by those around us, but negative experiences all too frequently embed themselves in our minds, forever pushing us inwards, unkindly holding us back. Coming Home warmly inspires the reader to look again, to see things differently, to address our fears and see our true selves, to be who we were meant to be. Being your true self is your gift to you.

Caroline Paige, Author of *True Colours*

'*Coming Home* aims to guide the reader on a spiritual journey to feel at peace with themselves and find true happiness. By sharing her personal experiences of trauma in earlier years, Gillian engages you from the start and gently encourages you on a path to self-awareness, showing you the importance of learning to live in the present without allowing the past to haunt you or being fearful of what the future may hold. I felt a lot of what she wrote resonated with me, as I am sure it will with many other people. Her empathy and optimism shine through her writing and she has inspired me to look a little deeper into the way I live my life and see the world. This is a touching and honest insight into how someone can be made to feel as a result of the cruelty of others and the lasting effects that cruelty can have. It is also a message of hope that there is a way to leave the demons of the past behind and achieve happiness and self-acceptance.'

Deborah Twelves, Author of *12 Years a Stranger*

'Not your typical "self-help" book! Gillian has a way of halting your own negative self-talk at any point in your journey and gently guides you back to the right path of being who you are authentically. A real reminder that you have more to offer our world if you are offering your true self.'

Ashleigh Macdonald, Choreographer and Administrative Manager, The Jungle Body Australia

Coming
Home

A Guide to
Being Your
True Self

GILLIAN
McMICHAEL

a R°think Press company

First published in 2022 by
Panoma Press Ltd
www.rethinkpress.com
www.panomapress.com

Book layout by Neil Coe

978-1-784529-70-3

Dedicated to you

Live life honouring the whole of you.

May this book give you everything you need to walk
yourself back home to your true self.

Contents

Introduction

They say in life that we all experience a spiritual awakening, but not all recognise it when it happens. My spiritual awakening happened over a decade ago, in 2010. I'd been married for nearly ten years; I had a successful business, and when the recession hit, the wheels started to come off. Not just with my business but in all aspects of my life. Within 12 months, I had almost lost everything. My home, my car, my marriage and my business were gone. This tsunami of events hit me full force and spat me out into a new world. A world I was not accustomed to or even familiar with. Alongside this, I was left with a debt of £97k that had to be paid back.

I was a coach. I helped others manifest their dreams; how could this have happened to me? Up until that point, I'd run a successful business, been a good wife and built a lovely home. But as I stood there holding my six-year-old son's hand with my life's possessions stuffed into a few suitcases, I questioned – what went wrong?

My reality was not what I had dreamed of, and at the age of 39, this was not the position I wanted to find myself in. I had no time to sit still and wallow. I didn't have a choice; I needed to survive. I couldn't sink, so I chose to swim. I had no idea what I was swimming towards, but I dived in and off I went.

I needed most of all to work. Without work I had no money, and that scared me to death. Like a woman possessed, I set off. I was a powerhouse of energy, drive and determination. I didn't stop to think; all I needed to do was to survive. A loan from my parents allowed me to get a rented apartment, a home for my son, not ours, but I knew it could be home. A borrowed car, which I am still forever grateful for, allowed me to take my son to his sporting activities, and playdates. This made life seem normal. A computer and a desk. I had to salvage some of what I'd lost. I pushed my fear, anger, pain and shame down into the depths of my belly and focused on what I knew best. Surviving.

With trepidation, I reached out to those clients who had been loyal and knew me most. I was honest but humiliated about sharing my story of liquidation and personal failure. But within a few months, one of those clients gave me an olive branch, and I went back to work. Self-employed with a new trading name. I did what I knew best, work hard, go the extra mile, deliver well, and put on a brave face. Regardless of how I felt inside.

Putting on a brave face was something I've done for most of my life. When I reflect on my childhood, I remember Sunday dinners, holidays, special occasions, routine, talks around the kitchen table, and a whole host of good family memories. But I also remember not fitting in, being bullied, emotionally blackmailed, protecting myself, no real true friends and loneliness. I've lived, like most, with conflicting opposites. A steady stream of mixed emotions. Happiness, sadness, softness, hardness, kindness, cruelty, light, dark, pleasure and pain. That steady stream of mixed emotions would always lead me to choppy waters. I would lose my footing and find myself adrift, saying and doing things that came from a place of anger, disappointment and frustration. All in service of self-protection.

This started when I was eight years old when I was first bullied at school. My harassment continued into my early twenties and caused me a lifetime of pain. This, I know now, was the moment when I became disconnected from myself and let go of the real me and instead painted on the brave face. Since then, I found myself swimming against the current, trying to swim upstream rather than going with the flow. I couldn't find my natural rhythm, so instead, I would battle my way through everything – surviving – until I was so exhausted, I wanted to give up. But instead, I would paint on the brave face in the hope no one would see what lay under the veneer.

There is only so much incongruence one can live with, and there will come a time when something bigger than yourself gives you a nudge. When I look back on my life, I had many nudges and many I ignored. Until that one day over a decade ago when I got a shove, pushed so far that I needed to pay attention and do something different. I had been stripped of all that I had.

Confused and in sheer panic I relied upon what I knew best: work hard, get your head down and hopefully over time things will work out. Which is what I did, but alongside that, something else was happening. I was waking up to something new inside me.

My narrative had always been strong, and I'd been playing the same tapes over and over in my mind for most of my life. I was sick of hearing them. *You're not worthy, you're not good enough, you don't belong, you're small, you are weak, you're stupid, you're a failure.*

I was these things. They were me. The trigger had been pulled, and now under my new circumstances, this narrative was even louder. I couldn't escape the voice that rattled my brain. I was sick of what it was doing to me, and I was frightened of who it would make me become.

I was functioning, but I was lost. I could barely recognise myself. I hadn't realised that I'd been playing roles for most of my life. All to aid my need to fit in, be liked and to belong. I'd accepted those roles and had played them well over the years. But now I had to do something different. I had to figure out who I was. The realisation of this crept up on me over the first months of my survival, but I didn't know what to do with this new awareness.

I wanted to carry on and suppress all of what I was feeling, push it back down into the depths of my being, but I couldn't. Pandora's box was open, and all my past came pouring out. I didn't know what to do with it all. I didn't really have time for it, but I couldn't shake it. It followed me around until I finally paid it the attention it wanted.

I gave in, stopped fighting it and started listening to a part of me that I never knew existed. I realised the shoes I'd been walking around in since I was eight years old were not mine; they had never fit. They were too tight, too restrictive, uncomfortable, yet every day, I had put them on and worn them until my feet ached, equally as much as my heart did.

I'd been walking around, living my life in those shoes for nearly 30 years. When the lights went out, and I lay staring at the celling engulfed by the dark, I decided enough was enough. I could no longer keep squashing my feet into those shoes. I needed to start wearing my own. I was compelled to find out who I was, what I wanted and what was my purpose. I wanted to discover what brought me joy, fulfilment and happiness. I wanted to be free from a life with conflicting opposites. I wanted to delete the tapes that had been playing non-stop in my mind. I wanted to create a new playlist, one that would bring me peace and inner happiness. I wanted to find a way to get to dry land, stop swimming against the current. To walk the path that I was meant to walk.

The immensity of what I desired was much bigger than saying enough was enough. It was huge and more challenging than I imagined. I was scared because once I took those shoes off, I didn't know who I would meet. Who would that person be stripped bare behind the painted on brave face? Who would I be with nothing masking who I was? I didn't recognise myself wearing others' shoes but would, could, I recognise myself without the things I had wrapped myself up in for 30 years?

I didn't know the answer to this, but I did know my feet needed to breathe, my body longed to wear my own outfits, my face didn't need to be painted any longer. My mind needed to quieten, and my heart needed to mend, and so for the first time in 30 years, I took the shoes off and stood barefoot.

After the panic had died down, the questions started to form. Who am I, what do I want? What is my purpose? As a transformational coach, I knew there had to be a reason for what had happened. There is always a reason and always a lesson to be learned. I just didn't know fully what that was. The one thing I did know for sure was that I needed to find myself. My true self.

In my moment of awakening, I was no longer engulfed by the dark. The light was on, and I could see clearly for the first time in over 30 years. So, I set out on a new journey. One that led me back home, back to my true self.

This book is written for you. I invite you to follow the steps that I took, taking each step carefully and with the intention of being open and willing to learn. I will share with you the journey I took to my self-discovery, which you can do too.

When you embark on this journey, I encourage you to see it as an adventure. An opportunity to explore with no major expectations of who you are and what your path should look like. It will all become apparent as you start to walk barefoot.

Like all journeys of self-discovery, you will take the scenic route, you will stop off at destinations that you like and enjoy exploring, and there will be other destinations that you feel quite the opposite, as you won't like what you see and how you feel. But it's important that you experience all aspects of this journey as otherwise, it won't be as enriching.

This book invites you to answer four questions:

1. Who am I?

2. What do I want?

3. What is my purpose?

4. What am I grateful for?

You will firstly be looking inward, secondly, focus outwards, thirdly, you will share what you know with others, and finally, you will experience deep gratitude when you arrive back home to your true self. I want you to experience this journey as it is meant to unfold, taking it step by step.

This journey will be transformational; you will, at times, have ups and downs. It may not always be easy, there will be bumps in the road, and it will, for sure, take you out of your comfort zone. But if you remain steady, with your bare feet on the ground, you will find your way home, back to your true self.

I invite you to learn how to embrace yourself, reconnect and re-establish who you are. As your guide, I hope that the lessons shared can help you heal and bring you closer to coming home.

I look forward to walking you back home, back home to your true self.

8

CHAPTER 1

Quietening The Mind

'Quiet the mind, and the soul will speak.'

Ma Jaya Sati Bhagavati

So where do we start? Taking that first step is always the hardest but once made, you will ask yourself, 'What took me so long?' So here we are at the beginning – the first step.

On this journey we must start with self-first, which means we have to look within. Any transformational journey has a dual aspect to it, and that's why we must start with learning to quieten the mind. Most of us spend our whole lives in activity, navigating the demands of a noisy and stimulating world. Even when we are in a completely quiet setting, you will find your mind full of thoughts about the past and plans for the future. If, like me, you will find yourself having a continual stream of interpretations and judgments about yourself and others. You will frequently review past stories and events you've experienced in your life. They will roll over and over in your mind until you can't remember what the truth of those experiences was.

Finding stillness within is not easy to do, especially in the world we live in today. Quietening the mind and trying to create stillness within is tricky. We can try and force things to slow down, switch off, to stop thinking, to stop analysing, but it's difficult to do. In fact, it is impossible to not have thoughts.

We have between 60-80,000 thoughts a day, meaning we experience 1.2 thoughts every second. So as long as you are breathing, you will have thoughts. Every thought you have has a beginning, middle and end. Yet, the thoughts we have today, we will have tomorrow and the day after, the week after, the month after, and so on. No wonder we're exhausted.

New thoughts will arise based upon our experiences, our patterns of behaviour and our external stimulus. These thoughts will drift in and out of our consciousness. Thoughts will disappear, some will be the same, and others will be new. Our thoughts are stored in our minds, and over time they turn into memories.

The world we live in is complex, challenging and complicated. Technology, for all its wonder, is drowning us and taking over our lives. With the constant need to follow each other, like and receive likes. The persistence to show others how happy we are by posting selfies. The desire to impress by how quickly we can respond to an email, text message, a friend request, a like, a post, and it goes on and on and on. None of this requires a quiet mind; in fact, the busier the mind, the quicker you are to get on and stay online.

Living life in this way means none of us live in the present or fully in the moment. When we do not live in the moment, it can lead to an imbalance, and that, in turn, can affect our physical, emotional and mental health.

Virtual connections can be useful, but not at the cost of losing the connection with yourself. Most of us have become comfortable with this way of living and what I would call 'role-playing,' pretending that life is awesome, having a huge following of friends, showing others how good you look, in forced poses, with fake smiles and showcasing where you are in the world, what you're doing and with who.

When we are in these spaces, we lose the true meaning of being connected and in the moment. Instead, our focus is on external validation and being wrapped up in what others think of us. All of this takes us further away from our true selves, and the only way we can get back to ourselves is by making the commitment to quietening the mind by finding stillness within.

If you genuinely want to come home to your true self, you need to stop focusing your attention on the outside world and turn your attention to what's going on inside. Most of us are conditioned to get on social media first thing in the morning, check our emails before we even leave the house and do the same before we go to bed, so it's no wonder we don't have the time or the capacity to be quiet and to be still.

It's difficult for anyone to get away from the world we live in unless you decide to isolate yourself from the outside world. The only way to do that would be to cut off all forms of communication and go and live like a hermit. Only a few can do this; most can't. So, we must find a way that allows us to connect at a deeper and authentic level with ourselves whilst living and fully functioning in the world we live in.

So, how do we move from activity into silence and in a way that works for you?

The most important habit I've formed in the last decade has been to learn how to meditate. I started off learning how to breathe consciously, which I realised I never did nor do many others in their day-to-day life. Breathing is something we all do daily. It is the first thing we do when we enter the world, and it will be the last thing we do before we leave. The body, in a living state, breathes involuntarily whether we are awake, sleeping, or actively exercising. Breathing is living. It is a vital function of life. In yoga, it is referred to as pranayama. 'Prana' is a Sanskrit word that means life force, and 'ayama' means extending or stretching. The word 'pranayama' translates to the control of life force.

Every cell in our body needs oxygen to function properly, and research has shown that regular practice of controlled breathing can decrease the effects of stress on the body and increase overall physical and mental health. Conscious breathing is essential when trying to quieten the mind as it allows us to connect in the moment with our breath. Inhaling and exhaling give us a centre point to focus, known as a 'drishti.' When focusing attention on our drishti, in this case, the breath, we connect in the moment to what's happening.

This can help to calm the mind, and after a few minutes of conscious breathing, you begin to find yourself moving from activity into silence. To do this well, we need to practise conscious breathing daily. Once you have mastered this, it is easier to transition into meditation.

Meditation will allow you to settle into quieter and quieter levels of awareness until you experience the pure silence within. Meditation has helped me over the years to become more peaceful, focused and calmer. I have also decreased my worry, stress and my levels of anxiety. I have become more appreciative and attentive to everything in my life. I am far from perfect, but it has helped me build a better relationship with myself. Most importantly, it has helped me understand who I really am.

Before I embarked on my own journey of self-discovery, I never paid too much attention to what I was doing or how I was doing it. Sometimes I would find myself on autopilot driving to work, wondering how I'd got there. There were times when I'd throw my dinner down my throat, barely taking time to recognise that I was eating. I was always dashing from one place to the other, always on the go in a constant state of panic or stress. My mind was never quiet, and I was never still.

Meditation calms your mind; it also calms your body and your emotions. In the process of going within. Meditation helps you to release accumulated tension, stress, fatigue, and everything that prevents you from experiencing your essential nature – your true self. Over regular practice, you restore the memory of who you really are.

Meditation is one of the most powerful practices for awakening your true self. And the peace that lies within. When in meditation, you go beyond the noisy chatter and chaos into inner quiet and expanded awareness. You begin to see that you are not your thoughts, emotions and the stories you tell yourself. When this happens, you can start to unfold your inner potential. Meditation allows us to be more effective, more creative, and every time you meditate, you unfold more and more of that potential and connect with who you really are.

Instead of being dominated by fear, guilt or judgment, you will find yourself in a quiet, steady state. From this state blossoms a sense of wellbeing and a feeling that you are safe.

When I learned to meditate, I was told that I was already enlightened, I was perfection, and in meditation, I didn't need to do anything apart from 'remember.' When I first heard this, I was like, no way, there must be more to it than this? But over the years, I was proven wrong; there isn't anything more to it. The thought of already being perfection took me a long time to understand and to believe.

The reason for this is because, like many, I was stressed; I was overloaded with life. I was crazy busy, too busy, juggling way too many balls and fighting too many fires. I was tired, deeply fatigued from years and years of prolonged tension and stress. I had no patience; I was short-fused, which meant my nervous system was overloaded too. This took me to places of frustration, anger and deep unhappiness. This had an impact on my diet, which led me to eating poorly, sleeping badly, and I was caught up in toxic relationships – mainly the one with myself. All of this hid the real me; it masked who I really was.

There is an intrinsic link between emotional pain, trauma, and continued high levels of stress, and if not managed, the emotions can start to manifest as physical symptoms of illness and imbalance in our bodies. Meaning without emotional wellbeing, we can't experience a healthy, vibrant life.

This is what happened to me. A year had gone by, and I was trying to balance paying off the debt, rebuild the business I'd lost, be a good mum, all whilst trying to figure out who I was. I found myself caught up in my own rat race. I was eating for quickness; I was heavier, my stomach more swollen. I remember going to a nutritionist as I couldn't shift any weight. They ran some tests, and I got told that my levels of cortisol were extremely elevated. This constant state of anxiety was, in fact, interfering with my body's ability to heal itself. In addition to all of this, I was told that I could be faced with mood swings, diabetes, and more severe mental and physical health issues if I didn't get on top of my stress. As I was leaving, he handed me a book on meditation and suggested I start to learn how to meditate.

I had no time to meditate. I was barely in the moment; I found it difficult to switch off. I was living my life in full flight or fight mode. I'd had a bad cold for months, brought on by being run down. I couldn't shift it. Once the coughing started, I couldn't stop, and within minutes I could barely breathe. I refused to pay attention, but as the morning went on, I realised I needed professional help. Gasping for breath, I was frightened to move; every time I did, the breathing got harder. I had a full-blown asthma attack even though I didn't have asthma. I could no longer keep up with the pace, and I needed to make a significant change to how I was living.

The consultant informed me I had developed adult asthma, and I needed three months of steroids and two inhalers to decrease the inflammation in my lungs. I had never suffered from asthma; why would I get this when I was 40? But I knew why. My body and mind were at an all-time low; my immune system had been under attack for years. I just needed a break from the work but also from the debt.

This was another nudge – and this time, I paid attention. I didn't like what I heard, but I needed to hear it. The consultant ran a series of tests, and I was told that my levels of cortisol were off the chart. This was not good. I had all the symptoms, weight gain, suppressed immune system, increased blood sugar levels and digestive problems. The message was simple, things have to change, or else you could be prone to diabetes, heart disease or even more significant illnesses. He asked how long I had been living this way. Too long was my reply. Way too long. As I was leaving, he suggested I learn to meditate. This was the second time I'd been told this in a matter of weeks. I needed to pay attention – the message could not have been clearer.

Meditation helped me settle my mind, settle my body, and with this, I got a deeper level of rest. Rest is how the body naturally heals itself. When the mind and body settle down, blockages, toxins, and emotional stresses start to unfold and release. These are released in an effortless manner. This allowed my heart rate to slow down, my blood pressure to normalise, and the deep-rooted stresses I had carried for most of my life to disappear.

It was like I had opened a doorway to a healthier and happier life. I felt alive, I was awake, and I started over the weeks, months and years to restore the memory of wholeness, of who I am.

I found that if I didn't meditate, my days didn't flow as much as they did when I meditated. I wasn't as focused or had the same clarity. I didn't have the same levels of energy or creativity. This led me to make a commitment to myself, it was more of a promise, and that was simply to meditate daily. No excuses.

A decade later, I've kept my promise, and I believe more than ever that meditation is the key that unlocks a busy mind, and through regular practice you can quieten your mind so you can find stillness within. You will notice that over time, your whole system – your body and mind will start to heal itself.

When I started to meditate, I wasn't quite sure what to expect. I was nervous as I wanted to immediately feel better. In all honesty, I wanted a quick fix. Now I know like anything in life, meditation and everything else I will share in this book is a journey. So, don't expect a quick fix. Don't get me wrong; you will start to feel different and notice you have a calmer outlook. But don't expect a full life transplant, as it won't happen in the way you expect it to.

At the beginning, I found myself falling asleep – a lot. For months, every time I meditated, I would be nodding off, my head bobbing and jerking all over the place. My arms, legs and shoulders would twitch. I later realised this was my body's way of releasing all the pent-up stress I'd been holding onto.

After several months, I stopped falling asleep and then came the torrid flow of words, thoughts, ideas, chatter, song lyrics, and conversations I'd had. The noise that I was hoping to stop came flooding in. It felt like I had turned on the tap, and I couldn't turn it off again. This was difficult as the whole purpose was to experience the opposite. When it did happen, it left me feeling disappointed in myself for not being able to meditate properly. I reached out to my meditation teacher, and he reminded me that in meditation, I needed to surrender, have no expectations. There were no good or bad experiences, it was just what it was. That was not what I wanted to hear at the time, but it was the truth. So again, I continued to practise, and with practice, I learned to let go of having any expectations when meditating.

All I needed to do was remember, just practise and be in the moment with it. I became, over time, mindful, knowing thoughts would always be there, but in that moment, when they arrived, I had a choice. Do I follow the thought, hold on to it and let it take me away or do I choose to let go of it in that moment, allow it to float away gracefully and come back to the breath? Over time I learned to let it float away gracefully. This was a regular dance I had with my mind when meditating. The key was to learn how to dance gracefully in the moment with your mind. Letting go and just be.

The more I did this, the more I settled into quieter and quieter levels of awareness until I'd experience the pure silence within. I was peaceful, focused and calmer in my daily life. My worry, stress and levels of anxiety drifted. I became more appreciative and attentive to everything around me. I was far from healed, but I started to build a better relationship with myself. I took myself off autopilot and got myself back behind my wheel.

In the process of going within, I began to release accumulated tension, stress, fatigue, and everything that was preventing me from experiencing my essential nature. Over time I began to see that I was not my thoughts, emotions, or the stories I had told myself. I still didn't know the answers to my questions, but I was awakening to my true self. I could feel the shift, slow and purposeful.

I found myself being ultra-effective, more creative, and I entered a quiet, steady state. From this state blossomed a sense of wellbeing and a feeling that I was safe. I no longer needed to keep protecting myself in the way I had before. I started to get comments from clients, colleagues and friends on how fresh I looked, how calm I seemed, how together I was.

I went back to the consultant a year later, pleased with my acquired meditation skills. We did the same tests, and when the results came back, he couldn't believe my body was naturally healing itself. The blockages, toxins and emotional stresses had been released. My heart rate had slowed down, my blood pressure normalised, and the deep-rooted stresses I had carried for most of my life were barely there. I felt alive; I was awake. Meditation unlocked my busy mind, and through the regular practice, I found stillness within.

In meditation, you may also experience pure silence, known as the 'gap.' As one thought finishes and another one is forming, there is space between those thoughts, and this is known as the gap. The gap is pure silence, infinite possibility; it's the moment when you connect to 'source'. There are many ways to describe source, such as 'god,' 'the divine' or the 'universe.' I wasn't sure what to call it. All I knew was that when this happened, I'd be surprised that my meditation practice was over.

What is source?

I believe source is where life originates from; it's the initiator of everything, intuition, guidance, inspiration, purpose and potential. My belief is that source is not external; in fact, it lies within each and every one of us. Going back to the phrase, you are perfection. This is source. Although you may be busy getting on with your life, source is within you. Like me, you may have forgotten how to connect with it.

When you connect to source, you tap into your intuition, your inner wisdom or divine guidance. Source allows you to remember, and if all we need to do in meditation is remember, then we have achieved what we have set out to do. The only problem is that you don't know you're in the gap, connected to source. You only realise this when you come out of it.

When I was first told about the gap, I was eager like most to fall into it. I had expectations of diving into this deep pool of perfection and would get to know everything about myself. Like Neo in the Matrix finding the Oracle. But the more I was consciously thinking about it, the less it happened.

When I learn something new, I always want to do it to the best of my ability. I am and always have been a conscientious student.

But with that comes a desire to please, to do it right and to get it right all the time. It also means I judge or criticise if I don't get the outcome I want. It was after many disappointing meditation sessions I realised that pushing for this to happen would only take me further away from what I wanted. Once again, I had to let go and how I meditated changed. It was more relaxed; I had a deeper sense of self and a connection to something bigger.

I accepted that I would not always slip into the gap, but when I did, when I would connect with source, to the field of silence and infinite potential, I could bring some of that back with me into my life. When you make the inner journey, slip into the field of silence, you reconnect with your essential nature, and you bring back a little of that silence and potential into all of your daily activities. For me, this meant in all of the chaos, complexity and pace of daily life I remained rooted in an underlying silence, stability and calm. I had the ability to think clearly and act consciously. I know when I access the field of infinite potential, I, too, am full of infinite potential. Anything is possible; you can walk your true path and live your life's purpose.

So why am I telling you all of this? Because to start this journey and to walk yourself back home to your true self, you have to learn to quieten your mind and learn to meditate.

To meditate, all you need to do is sit comfortably, close your eyes and make sure that you won't be disturbed by others. Ideally, you should meditate first thing in the morning before you fully engage with external activity and for no longer than 20–30 minutes a day. Thirty minutes? Yes, that sounds a lot now, but over time that's what you should be aiming for. But for now, especially if you are new to meditation, try and do it for a few minutes a day and then, over time, increase your meditation practice. You notice the word is practice. Practice is all it is, and with practice, we should have no expectation apart from practice.

To get into a meditative state, you first need to breathe consciously. To pay attention to your breath. To prepare yourself to consciously breathe, you simply connect to your breath and allow your awareness to move within. Be aware of your breath; notice the breath flow effortlessly. Inhaling and exhaling, just breathing in and breathing out with the natural ebb and flow of your body.

As thoughts arise, let them float away. Focus on your breath and connect in that moment with who you are. Know that between every thought is the gap, that space. All the creativity, happiness, joy and all the possibilities in your life come from that space. Allow your thoughts to settle down, allow your body to settle down and allow space to be created within you.

Maybe you can try it now. Firstly, sit comfortably with your back resting against something solid; you can either sit crossed-legged on the floor or in a chair that supports your back. Place the palms of your hands upwards, facing towards the sky, resting them on your lap or knees. Close your eyes and put your attention, your focus on your breath. Allow the breath to be relaxed, and inhale and exhale, just breathing in and breathing out through your nose. Keep your lips closed and relax your shoulders, jaw and brow. Do this for a couple of minutes and just be in the moment with the natural ebb and flow of your body. Deepening and lengthening the breath, inhaling and exhaling.

So how was it?

Remember, thoughts will arise, but if you continue to practise conscious breathing, you will start to experience inner silence and feel more peaceful. It is the space that comes with conscious breathing and meditation that you will need on this journey.

Meditation has been the greatest gift I have given myself. I know if you learn to quieten your mind and meditate too, it will be the same for you. I invite you to learn how to meditate so you too can reap the rewards of finding stillness within and connecting to source. This first step is essential to you returning home, back to your true self.

Exercise

Practise meditation daily, starting small with two minutes of conscious breathing. Inhaling and exhaling through the nose, with your lips closed. Remember to relax your jaw and brow and make sure you are sitting comfortably. If thoughts arise, choose to let them drift away and come back to the breath.

As you progress each week, add another one or two minutes to your practice.

It is best that you do this every day at the same time. It needs to become a daily routine. Please don't give up; remember you cannot fail in meditation. It is what it is; there is no good or bad. It is, however, a lifelong practice, but once you get into a routine and commit to that routine, you will start to cultivate a practice that works for you.

8

CHAPTER 2

Who Am I?

'Knowing others is wisdom, knowing yourself is enlightenment.'

Lao Tzu

Another year had passed, and I was still searching for answers. Who am I? What do I want, and what is my purpose? I decided to focus on one question at a time. These were big life questions and too big to answer all at once. I was meditating, and my life had somewhat calmed down. However, I was still busy as my debt was always present, reminding me of what had happened.

When we lead busy lives, it leads to being time poor. We stop focusing on our needs and desires. We become distracted, caught up in others' lives, spending most of our time playing catch up and losing ourselves in the void of doing. The to-do list never gets fully scored off, and instead, a new list longer than the day before emerges, and we become stuck. Caught on that hamster wheel, doing, doing, doing – otherwise known as groundhog day. Waking up to the same challenges, the same feelings and the same questions being posed. For me, it was: *There's got to be more to life than this. What am I meant to be doing?*

When we lose ourselves, we don't just forget who we are; we start to live a life that is not fully our own. We accommodate, we compromise, and we ignore. We delude ourselves into believing that if I just get through the next couple of weeks, I will get back to me being more like myself. *It's just busy… I just need to get through this week… I need to have that conversation, but I can do that tomorrow when I'm feeling more like myself.*

The list of excuses could go on forever, and they often do. Which means we get further and further away from who we really are. That was me, lost out at sea. My first recollection of this is when I was a child, then a teenager and finally as an adult. In fact, I'd been searching for the answer to 'Who am I?' for most of my adult life, searching for something but not knowing what I was looking for. In my moment of awakening, I knew I needed to find the answer, but I couldn't quite catch it, grab hold of it. When I thought I'd found it, it always slipped through my fingers.

I had moved from job to job, friendship group to friendship group, city to city, all in search of something I couldn't quite articulate. I found love, lost love. I recreated myself numerous times, and in all of this, I still felt something was missing deep within me. I wanted to know my truth, but I just couldn't get close enough to figure it out.

I realised that in my relationships at work, my friendships and at home, I had accommodated and compromised on nearly everything. I never said what I wanted or what I needed. I'd given away my personal power, and instead, I had become passive – a passenger in my own life. Being passive was something I never thought I would be, yet I seemed to accept it. I would sacrifice my own preferences and needs so that I could help others meet theirs. The voice I was speaking with was a diluted version of myself.

Over the years, I'd played many roles, some of them I'd put myself forward for and others I'd not. The roles I played had stuck, the dutiful daughter, the big sister, the accommodating girlfriend, the wife, the mother, the conscientious student, the gregarious friend, the quiet employee, the 'challenging' teenager.

These roles and labels I'd attached to myself or allowed others to attach them to me made me realise that I was lost. When I asked myself the question 'Who am I?', I couldn't answer. All that came out were the labels, the roles and the personas I had played since being a little girl.

I'd lost myself because I was a person who wanted to be accepted and liked. I needed to fit in; I was desperate to fit in. I'd been bullied in school. It started when I was eight years old and lasted until my early 20s. I got called 'Concorde' due to the size of my nose. The whole class would duck down in case my nose hit them as I entered the room; this became a frequent and long-standing event. As the teacher wrote on the blackboard, I would be thrown paper planes. People wrote notes about me; some I would see, others would be passed behind my back. Kids can be cruel, and this is where I started to cultivate one of my many roles. I pasted on a layer of protection and started to construct my armour. This armour was tough; once that was around me, I could play my role. 'The tough kid,' 'the outsider.'

Being an outsider was something I became. I don't believe that I was meant to live my life on the outskirts, but it's somewhere I found myself. I don't believe this was my doing fully, but I do know I was responsible for how long I remained on the sidelines. I spent over 30 years being a bystander, an onlooker, not once feeling I belonged.

Throughout these teenage years, I found myself drifting from one friendship group to the other, none really lasting any longer than a few months. I couldn't quite tell if this was my inability to trust, to settle and feel part of something. Or was it being driven by the group's choice? All I knew was I still felt like an outsider, looking in on the activities, the intimate conversations and friendships that had formed.

As a teenager, I would head up to my room where posters of Andrew McCarthy and Rob Lowe decorated my walls. These faces looked on as I became critical and judgmental of how I looked. I would, in the beginning, imagine my face different, without the big nose, with a face not as round, I wanted to be taller, thinner, better looking. I thought if I looked better, I would be liked, accepted, and I would belong. Over these years, my hair changed multiple times; I got a perm, it was highlighted, blonder, a new bob, a fringe. All to keep trying to look better, hoping that every time I changed my image, I would fit in, be liked, and the name-calling would stop. My fashions also matched my hair, and I was swept away with teenage girl coming-of-age films, *Pretty in Pink*, *Flashdance*, *The Breakfast Club* and *Dirty Dancing*. I related so much to the characters of these girls, equally struggling to fit in, but I related most to Baby in *Dirty Dancing*, she had a nose like mine too, and she got Johnny's attention. I remember sitting in the cinema watching *Dirty Dancing*, and my mum leaned over and said, 'Oh, she has a look of you, look, her nose has a bump in it, just like yours.'

I think it was supposed to help, to make me feel better in some way. But it didn't because no one was coming to my rescue, no one was going to say, 'Nobody puts Gillian in a corner.' In fact, I felt so far in the corner I didn't even know how to get out of it. The bullying continued; as I grew, so did the number of comments.

Keeping myself safe meant I learned to live within the lines. These lines kept me safe, kept me secure and steady as I navigated myself through the latter parts of my senior school education. I pretended that all the name-calling, the bullying, the whispering and laughing behind my back didn't matter. I would act, my newfound skills gave me an air of confidence, but if you scratched the surface, you would see it was fake. I trained myself to be numb, to cut out the noise and instead laugh along with them until they got bored and moved on to something else. The thing was, they never seemed to get bored, and I never could cut out the noise.

When in the lines, I could join in and speak up but only within the lines. My conformity to operate in this way was compounded with one thing only – collusion. I had become the conspirator in my own life. I played a role at school and a role at home. Whenever I was asked if I was OK, my response, canned, was always the same, 'I'm good, thanks; what about you?'

This is where I started to cultivate another of my many roles that I took with me into my adulthood. I became a chameleon. I learned to change my personality depending upon the groups of people I attached myself to. The more I did this, the more I pretended I was OK. But the more detached I became and the further away I got from myself. I chose to keep everyone at arm's length; I would not let anyone in. My outer shell hardened as it masked my vulnerability. I didn't realise it at the time because all I was doing was trying to fit in, belong, and, more than anything, protect myself from getting hurt.

As humans, we all want to fit in, to belong and to be liked. We don't really want conflict; we want harmony. We want life to be easy, not difficult, and most of us do this at the expense of losing our true selves.

When we choose to play a role or happily attach a label to ourselves, we are usually hiding something from the outside world. We are complex beings; there is always a reason for that hidden side of ourselves or the reason why we choose to hide it in the first place. I know, now, that I was hiding my vulnerability, my hurt, pain, humiliation and shame. I could never share this as I would appear weak.

As always in life, there is a pivotal moment, a life-changing event. A traumatic event that thrusts you into a place of vulnerability. Mine was when I was 16 years old. I'd been in the school Christmas play, playing Dorothy, the lead character in *Gregory's Girl*, an outsider who played football and was finally accepted by her fellow school friends. And then it happened in real life. The group of older girls who were in the play asked if I wanted to go out with them. I couldn't believe it. They asked me. I had to control my tears and steady myself. This was unheard of, but yes, I wanted to go.

My dreaming of this time was now happening, and eager to fit in, I spent most of Saturday afternoon walking around the shops trying to get an outfit to meet the expectations of my new older friends. It needed to be cool, as I needed to fit in. It took me three hours to get ready; my brother laughed as he looked on at all my preening and painstaking fussing over what lipstick was best to wear. I was giddy on a cocktail of nerves and excitement. I was dropped off at the meeting point by my mum, who told me no drinking was allowed. I was OK with that as I'd never drunk alcohol before. I could see the older girls at the bar; they were ordering cider and black. I stood next to them and ordered a Diet Coke. They looked on, smirking, but no one said anything at the bar. Once we all had our drinks, the gang moved through the sea of bodies to the back room. I heard the older boys were in the back room. My heart now racing, I followed.

The girls, flicking their hair, laughing loudly, looking over their shoulders to see if any of the boys were looking over. One of the group asked me to move further into the back room, which meant me standing in the middle of the room where all the boys were. One of them quickly nudged the others, and as I smiled at them, they all stared until one of them shouted, 'Bing Bong, ladies and gentlemen, Concorde is landing, duck before she knocks your drinks over' and with that, every single one of them ducked. They all crouched down under the table their beers rested on. Hyena type laughing surrounded me, I felt dizzy, and the metallic taste of bile was in my mouth. I was going to be sick; I had to get out of there. When I looked up to my newfound girlfriends, they, too, were in hysterics. Between their laughter, I could hear, 'That's so awful, but how funny is Jason; he is such a laugh.' Every time I looked around, everyone who was sitting in the back room ducked. I was frightened to move my head in case another group of people ducked down. I was mortified; I froze, and I didn't know what to do. Tears ready to spill over. The laughter had grown into something new. It was savage. I gingerly walked through the crowded main bar until the girls couldn't see me any longer, and I sneaked out onto the main street.

Holding back all my emotion until I was out of hearing distance, I screamed. The noise that came out was something I never knew existed within me. Years of pain, humiliation and degradation spewed out of me. The public shaming had marked me for life. The mortification, disgrace and embarrassment shook me to the core. I headed home disillusioned and even more lost. Unable to get a firm footing, something had changed within me. I was no longer the same.

When I arrived home, I took a gulp of my dad's brandy from the drinks cabinet and waited.

It was in that waiting I decided I wanted a nose job. Something had to be done to stop this. It was the only thing I could think of. It was drastic enough; it was desperate enough, and it would stop them. They couldn't call me Concorde anymore if I didn't have a big nose. My parents eventually gave in after months of me wearing them down. I was so grateful. I believed that all would be well, I'd come back to the sixth form with a new nose, and everyone would accept me. I would look different, they wouldn't know why, but they would like me. Like how I looked, and I'd be included in the inner circle. My life from this point would be full of fun, happiness and opportunity. This would be my happy ending. My 16-year-old brain working overtime, dreaming of a life of what could be.

My delusion didn't last long; the small town knew everything. As I lay in my hospital bed, nose packed with cotton wool, eyes blackened and swollen, I peered through to see the face of one of my worst offenders bringing me some tea and toast. One of the class bullies. This was supposed to be part of my recovery; if I could eat the toast and drink the tea, I could go home and start living my life, my new life. But here she was, as she leaned over to put the light refreshments in front of me, she smiled, grabbing my chart and said loudly, 'Rhinoplasty, mmm interesting.'

Before I got home, everyone I knew, knew. Patient confidentiality had been breached, and there was no going back. As my fractured nose healed, my belief in the human spirit shattered. There was nothing I could do; I hated where I lived and the people who lived there.

I arrived back at school, I'd lost weight, my nose was new, my style was new, but inside I was still the same, and so was everyone else. The external façade was just window dressing. The reality of my world took its place. As I entered the rec room, everyone ducked in preparation in case my nose knocked them over.

As I transitioned into my adulthood, I became a shell of who I was; my confidence dipped, my self-belief disappeared. I stopped going for the things I wanted and became a passive passenger in my own life. I allowed myself to drift further and further away from the real me. I became the supporting actor in my life, instead of remaining the star of it.

I played all my roles perfectly; I was a conscientious student. In my relationships, my passiveness made it difficult for me to say no. I justified everything I did by qualifying everything I said. I would start my sentences with, 'Would you mind if...' or, 'Is it OK with you if I...'

I was always seeking approval and the go-ahead from others. When there was conflict, I would become subdued. I let others verbally take the lead or control the conversation, even if I didn't agree. I never owned my opinions. I would change my mind, my thoughts, and my viewpoint as quickly as the wind changed direction. I believed my views didn't matter, and I stopped sharing them. My narrative became, 'I don't mind what we do, you choose.' I lived within the lines, and I conformed to what I thought people wanted from me. I restricted myself fully from being myself.

When you're adrift like this, all kinds of emotions arise, lack of worthiness, weakness, sadness, failure, stupidity and bitterness. For me, all these feelings were led by fear.

When fear is present, it will hold you tightly in its grip until you succumb, so you keep accommodating your needs. You compromise on your desires, ignore your strengths and talents, and finally trick yourself into believing you don't have a choice. And that's what I did. Until that day when I was forced to pay attention. In all honesty, my awakening happened abruptly and came 23 years after my pivotal moment. Things were out of my control, and I was forced to stop. The role-playing, the labels had not been serving me well. I had to find the courage to answer that question, 'Who am I?'

After months of trying to get myself back on my feet, when the anger and pity for myself had subsided, I stood looking at myself in the mirror, and I didn't know who was looking back at me. I didn't even recognise myself or even the roles I'd been playing. In the starkness of my reality, the world I'd created crumbled. The armour I'd lathered on over the years started to crack, and the walls I'd built shook. The only thing I did know was that I had to choose, do I sink even further and lose every part of me, or do I swim? Swimming I was familiar with, but I was in unchartered waters, and I didn't know what would happen. The one thing I did know was if I could let go of who I thought I should be and instead look with fresh eyes, then maybe I would find my answer.

When I looked in the mirror, all I kept hearing was, 'Who am I?' At first, I couldn't bear to look, but for some reason, I kept getting drawn back to the mirror and that question, 'Who am I?'

Being able to articulate who you are takes time; it requires a robustness and inner strength. You must learn to trust yourself. I didn't trust myself, yet I knew I had to dig deep and rebuild.

I couldn't keep taking a fleeting glance in the mirror each morning, frightened to see who would be looking back; I had to look for longer. It required courage to really see me, for who I was – warts and all. The good and the bad.

When I stood in the mirror, owning all of who I was, things started to emerge. I still had the external labels such as I am a mum, a friend, a daughter, a sister. But there was something more unearthing within. To truly find out who I really was, I needed to answer the soulful question, 'Who am I?'

I kept asking the same question, and over time, I began to give myself permission to look underneath the surface. I needed to go beyond the external and connect with the inner me. This was the first step in learning how to trust myself. I longed to free myself from the roles I'd played and the labels others had attached to me. I no longer wanted to be a diluted version of myself. I did not want to be a passive passenger in my life any longer, and so I chose to explore and find out my truth. Who am I?

When you do this, you begin to gain clarity, the fog lifts, and you start to get closer to your real self. You start to see yourself not for who you have become but for who you truly are. It took me months of daily questioning to articulate my truth.

So, what happens when we drop those associations, the roles and labels?

It's like peeling away the layers of an onion. The more layers you peel away, the closer you get to your true self, to the core of who you are.

When I asked, 'Who am I?', I was a mum, a wife, a friend, a daughter, a businesswoman, a sister and a granddaughter.

So, I asked again, 'Who am I?', This time came facts and figures: I am British, I'm an Aries, I'm 41 years old.

Then followed qualities such as I'm a good daughter, a good mum, a kind person. I am funny. I am a good listener.

I moved through a series of labels and roles to which I hadn't even realised I was attaching myself. I had to go deeper to peel away all the layers of the onion – the more I asked, the more I got to know myself – this spurred me on.

When I asked myself for the twelfth time, 'Who am I?', my response finally was, 'I am me,' and then there was silence. I had stripped away all that I needed to. The silence was profound because in that silence came a fresh energy and eagerness to connect with my true self. The problem was I didn't know who that 'me' was, but I was excited to reacquaint myself.

Exercise

To help you master this lesson, sit in front of a mirror and set a timer for 30 minutes. Take some time to connect to your breath. Place both feet on the ground and rest both hands on your lap, so you settle into yourself. When you have done two minutes of breathing, open your eyes and take a good look at the reflection in front of you. Who do you see?

Take time to look at your face, your features, your eyes, nose, hair and lips. Notice who is looking back at you without being critical of yourself or finding fault. Look to truly see who you are. Every couple of minutes, ask yourself, 'Who am I?'

Ask yourself the question 12 times. Each time writing down the answer you get. Remember, you will get different answers to me, but keep asking until you get to your core. I encourage you to peel away any protective layers you have wrapped around you. Stand in the mirror and take a good, long look.

Write down all the labels you and others have given you; keep asking yourself, 'Who am I?', and see what emerges.

CHAPTER 3

Being True To Myself

'Be Congruent. Be Authentic. Be Your True Self'.

Mahatma Gandhi

Once I had the words, I needed to figure out what they meant to me and how I could live my life being me. I had no idea how or what that would look like.

When I thought about the statement 'I am me', the desire to be true to it rippled through every part of my body. I repeated the statement out loud several times a day, and words appeared, such as integrity, living life to my beliefs, living my values, being honest, sincere, whole, authentic, fulfilled and happy all came to mind. I knew these were all good words to use, but how was I going to live it? I wanted so much to live my life honouring this, but I couldn't figure out how.

Being true to yourself starts with knowing who you are and accepting yourself fully. It's important that you can articulate what your truth is. What defines you and what makes you whole. Being true to yourself is a personal choice and one that revolves around making decisions on how you want to live your life. Who you want in your life, and how you want to be spending your time. We all have the power to live our lives in a way that is meaningful and true to us.

When you start to embark on a journey to understand what being true to yourself means, fear can creep in. When fear is present, we can put roadblocks in our way. These roadblocks manifest in different guises. They can be little white lies you tell yourself or others, such as answering the question 'How are you?' with 'I'm good, I'm fine' when you're not; or when invited to come out for a drink, saying 'I can't; I have to work late' when you don't, or even 'OK, sure, that sounds like a great night', even though you don't want to go. Or they can be ingrained beliefs that make it difficult to appreciate you have a choice. Most humans, if not all humans, have at least one ingrained belief that makes it difficult to move beyond the constraints of our minds.

We believe that if we are true to ourselves, we will let people down. People may not like us. We often see being true to ourselves as a big task – we're too busy or don't have the time – and this can become our excuse. *Will I still be liked, and will I belong?* The question 'What will people think of me?' and, more than anything, 'What happens if I fail at this?' come from your passive passenger voice. The one that wants you to remain in your comfort zone to keep you safe. This passive passenger voice is the ego, one that we all have. You will notice the ego has many voices. As we go through this journey together, you will get to know the ego and when it is present. Regardless of how it presents itself, it is there. We just need to figure out how to manage it. In this case, it's the voice that tells you it's OK to keep playing the roles and to keep hold of the labels because it's what you know; it's familiar. Familiarity gives us great comfort, and if we allow it, it will keep us locked into the same pattern of behaviour and the same belief systems.

I was teaching about being true to yourself on one of my coach training programmes, and a student challenged me: 'How can you be true to yourself when you're in a relationship, have a family and have responsibilities – you can't just go off and throw caution to the wind – you know, do whatever you like?'

In the real world, none of us can walk away from our responsibilities, but you do have a choice about being truthful in how you feel about them and how you want to live within them. If you deny how you feel, you are ignoring your basic need to be yourself. You are blocking your human right to self-expression.

Most of us sacrifice our need to be true to ourselves because we want to fit in, conform and be accepted by others. We all have the need to belong; our sense of belonging can sometimes be so strong that we start to please others and ignore our own needs and desires.

People pleasing is the biggest factor in stopping us from being our true self. The need to fit in, be part of something, follow the crowd, be accepted by others, all lead to us forgetting about who we really are, and instead, we succumb to the needs of others. When you do this, you dilute your personality, and you are immediately limiting your potential. This moves you further away from finding true happiness and fulfilment. In fact, it brings you nothing but inner conflict.

Inner conflict is one of the biggest struggles humans experience in their lifetime. It can be a lifelong battle that messes with your mind, your emotions and stops you from accomplishing anything you desire. Inner conflict resides in your mind, although you may feel it in your body. Our mind gives us opposing motivations based upon conflicting beliefs, needs and wants. These arise and create dilemmas, and these dilemmas create turmoil within: 'Should I, shouldn't I?', 'Can I, can't I?', 'Yes, no' or 'It's good, it's bad', 'I will, I won't.'

Our mind has a way of dominating us; in these moments of conflict and confusion, we lack equanimity. Meaning we don't have balance between the heart and head. Your heart says one thing, 'I want to be true to myself,' and your mind says another, 'You can't change your career at 40, because you're too old.'

I needed to empty my baggage, get it all out on the table for me to see what I needed to get rid of and what I wanted to keep. I had built some new habits, ones that would serve me well, but the remains of the past lurked in the shadows. It was about time they stood in full daylight so I could really see what I'd been carrying around with me.

I allowed the students to explore and discuss in their groups their perspectives on the concept and what it meant to them. As they discussed, debated and concluded their take on the subject, I wrote down what it meant to me.

I'd been telling myself all sorts of lies. Contradictions, incongruent statements. Some of these were to protect myself and others just because it's what I knew. It was easier to pretend rather than be honest about how I really felt.

I found it difficult being honest with myself. I was masking my vulnerability, how exposed I really felt and how scared I was of failing again. Fear crept in; a silent assassin ready to cull its target when not looking. I was in constant conflict with myself. I was my hero but also my villain. In my need to push on, to overcommit and overdeliver, I was limiting myself. I was repeating the same patterns of my previous behaviours. The dance so familiar I didn't even need to think about the steps.

My mind played tricks on me, I wanted to be true to myself, but I had no idea how to go about it. My confusion within brought a lack of clarity. I just couldn't get the balance right between what my heart longed for and what my head told me. I needed to resolve this conflict within. I needed to figure out how to be true to me and sustain it.

I posed myself several questions:

- *What would 'being true to myself' mean?* It would mean I could express myself and be clear about my needs and wants. My desires, aspirations and my feelings could be shared. I would not feel the need to hide them or suppress them any longer. If I was true to myself, I could live my purpose, really show up and be present in my life.

- *If I was true to myself, what would I let go of?* My own judgments; the assumptions I was making about myself and others.

- *If I were true to myself, what am I afraid might happen?* I wouldn't like who I become; I may continue to be an outsider. I would not be brave enough to honour myself in this way.

- *How would being true to myself change my life?* I would be free; I could be myself and I would find peace within.

- *What am I learning about myself?* Being true to myself is not selfish. It is self-care and, more than anything, I needed to care for myself. How could I be good with others if I couldn't be good with myself? I knew if I were to speak my truth, I would embrace all of me.

The word 'surrender' kept coming into my thoughts, something I had been taught in meditation. If I let go of the expectations I have for myself, then I could let go of the expectations and thoughts others had of me. I would not be influenced by others' thoughts, in who I am and how I should be living my life. Being true, speaking my truth would change my life. I knew it; I believed it. The path I'd walk would be the one I was meant to be on. The work I'd do would be the work I was meant to do. I knew this deep within my core. I believed that my fear, anxiety and worry would dissolve. I was determined for congruence. For my truth.

My emotional self-care was now a must. I had to get to the root cause of my conflict. If I could start to speak up, say what I wanted and needed, I could hopefully stop being a passive passenger in my life. I could step up and take responsibility for who I was and who I would become.

I had started to learn the power of choice. I had always been one of those people who answered a question with a question. When asked, 'What do you want for your dinner?', I would reply, 'What do *you* want?'; in answer to 'What movie shall we see?' I'd say, 'What movie do *you* want to see?' The answer was always a question. I needed to move on from being passive. I wanted to speak up, make choices. I just hadn't done so for such a long time.

I started to test out choice, cognitively I knew I'd always had a choice, but when caught up in my drama, I hadn't aligned myself to that concept. It always felt there wasn't a choice, but as I leaned into choice, I felt empowered, liberated; I had options. I started to build my strength in this new muscle, and over time, I started to make choices that were true to me. I tested this out at home. It felt forced to begin with, but after a while, it started to feel OK.

At work, it was a little different. I got resistance; the team didn't quite like it when I said no to something. It surprised me, and it made me question what kind of leader was I? The team were performing well, but I realised I was also a passive leader. I allowed them to do what they wanted in many ways. My need to have no conflict meant that I let them set their own rules and ways of working. I dressed this up as, *I was leading them by coaching,* but in all honesty, I chose the easy option as I didn't want to deal with conflict.

The business was growing; it was a small team, which also meant the environment was more lenient. But when I had to challenge performance or behaviours, I would leave it too long, and the power of the discussion was lost. I would always back down; sometimes, I'd contradict myself.

When I eventually started saying no to requests at work, some of the team didn't like it. But I remained steady in my truth. I knew I was doing the right thing, not just for me but for the team and for the business. The focus was no longer blurred; it was sharp, and out of this came a new vision for Full Circle. The unrest continued, but the more I stayed true to my thoughts, feelings and actions, the more the team settled.

This was quickly followed by me speaking my truth in all situations. If I spoke my truth, I would be able to say how I feel and express what I need. I would be not only truthful with myself, but I would also be truthful with others. Finally, I would be able to accept my truthful self. I would not be afraid of the person staring back at me in the mirror. Or feel the need to change, just to fit in. Instead of looking and not seeing, I would see my truth. As I did this, I found it difficult not to be true to myself. My truth seemed to be everywhere, in every conversation, in every situation. I invited it in. My truth was a welcomed guest, and one I knew would never outstay its welcome.

Exercise

The first step is to understand what being true to yourself means to you. Each one of us will answer these questions differently. Please do not judge yourself as you answer these questions. Please go beyond the normal surface answers and allow your truth to come out.

Remember, it is easy to assume being true to yourself is selfish and self-centred. In fact, being true to yourself is about self-care. Being true to yourself is a commitment; like most things, you have to work at it every day and make sure you are honouring yourself and your own truth. You need to listen to your truth and have the courage to speak it out loud.

Consider the following statements and questions:

- Being true to yourself would mean…

- If you were true to yourself, you could…

- If you were true to yourself, you would let go of…

- How would being truer to yourself change your life?

- If you were true to yourself, what are you afraid might happen?

- What are you learning about yourself?

CHAPTER 4

Making Meaning

'What we think, we create; what we feel, we attract; what we imagine, we become.'

Buddha

I took my three promises with me everywhere I went. I wrote them on Post-it notes and had them stuck to my fridge door. I even had them on scrap bits of paper that I carried with me in my purse:

I embrace the truth in the present moment.

I will speak my truth.

I accept my truth.

I forced myself to read them daily until I knew them off by heart. But I needed to do more than just remember them; I needed to truly make meaning of them and to make them meaningful in my life. This concept was the most stretching of all. I was getting to know myself at a much deeper level. I was reconnecting and getting familiar with who I was and what I wanted, so I could live a fulfilled life. I was now 44 years old.

To get closer to your core self, your truest self, you need to connect with yourself at a deeper level. This will generate more self-awareness and knowing. This knowing, in turn, will be your guiding light as you move forward into the next phase of your journey. But to gain that deeper self-awareness, you must explore the way you make meaning in your life. In your conversations with yourself and with others. How you express what's really happening, how you genuinely feel and why you make the choices you do. Meaning making helps us respond to others and situations rather than react. It will help you understand how you experience your life, how you can let go of unresolved issues and past experiences.

To do this, we need to learn the difference between perception and reality. By knowing the difference, we can shift our perceived reality into our actual reality. We all have perceptions about things in our lives and in our relationships. These perceptions tend to always be about ourselves and about the way we think others perceive us. These perceptions are how our opinions form, the way we see things and the way we experience things.

A perception can be regarded as an impression that resides in the memory of an experience we've had, and that experience is imprinted. These impressions remain; they form strong bonds within our ego. As we grow, they grow until we're unable to know what's real or what's a perception. An impression of something we think we have experienced. Another way of describing a perception could also be a mindset; how you view yourself and the world. We take for granted these perceptions. We don't question them; we just take them on board, and they become our reality.

But we can't accept that on this journey. We need to make meaning of how we feel and what we say so that we move beyond the principles of being true to ourselves to truly live our truth.

Our mind is beautiful, but it holds so much information we can sometimes feel overwhelmed with it all. Over two million years ago, our brains were approximately 400–550 cubic centimetres in size, and since then our brains have tripled in size. Tripling the brain size has provided us with the memory capacity that was essential for developing abstract thinking and language. This then moved on to reasoning, mathematics and the wider system of communication we are familiar with today. Our minds have the capacity to store information for more than a century. Automatically cataloguing, re-filling, and editing as needed. Although this is amazing, it can have its challenges, especially when trying to manage the stress, the worry and the over-thinking we find ourselves doing today. It will also stop us from living our truth.

Going back to those 60–80,000 thoughts a day, the ones that drift in and out of our consciousness will determine our perceptions. Thoughts will disappear; some will be the same as the day before. Some may linger and keep popping back into our consciousness, and others will be new, based upon the new experiences, situations or interactions we have. Our thoughts are stored, and over time they turn into memories. Not all thoughts are turned into a memory, but the thoughts that have feelings attached to them transition into something bigger, and that's when they become a memory.

Once a thought becomes a memory, our mind can influence how we feel. It can take us back to past experiences good or bad, it can trick us into thinking that what we're experiencing today is exactly what we experienced years ago. It can also determine how we react to situations based upon these memories today and in the future.

Another way to describe it is that the mind is the software to our soul. That software has been programmed since the day we were conceived. When we start to cognitively remember, recognise and feel the experiences we've had, our mind chooses to store these in our software.

All this programming leaves an imprint that creates a pattern that influences our behaviour. These imprints will simply either have a positive or negative impact on you. The mind sorts these experiences into good, bad, funny, happy or sad moments and these shape who we are and how we live our lives. These are the stories that we tell ourselves, our families, friends and colleagues.

The stories we share with others will always have emotions attached to them. When we share these stories, our emotions are easily brought back to the surface. Depending on how many times we discuss or share that particular story the emotions and the story gather momentum. They become much larger than they were when first experienced. These stories are exaggerated, adding two and two together and making five – this is what our software does. It colludes, it interprets, it manifests in ways that don't serve us well or in ways that are not always the truth. Instead, a perception is born, and the reality or separation of the truth in the situation is disregarded.

Let me introduce you to the concept of the software of the soul in a different way. If you think about it software is everywhere, we have it in our computers, our smartphones, iPads etc., and for thousands of years, the soul has had its own software. Another way of describing this is our habits; the software is our habitual way of living. This software has been built up over the years and can keep us in a holding pattern – thinking, behaving and feeling – even if the software is not working for us, we will keep repeating the same patterns.

In our software, we have action, memory and desire. The choices we make are based upon our actions, memories and desires. We take an action; this creates a memory. The memory creates a desire, and the desire leads, in turn, to another action. This is what we can refer to as the software of the soul.

So, if I perform an action, it will create a memory that then leads to a desire.

Let me give you an example of how this works.

Imagine I've never had a cup of coffee before. My colleagues are telling me how good it tastes, smells and how much energy it will give me. So, the next day when I'm heading to work, I pass a coffee shop, and I remember what my colleagues had told me. I go into the cafe and buy a cup of coffee; this is now the action. I now know what coffee tastes like, and I like it (they were so right) – it smells good and tastes good and then later in the day, I have more energy, and a memory is created. So, when I walk past the coffee shop the next day, my memory kicks in and now creates a desire. That desire is to go back and have another coffee which then leads to another action.

So, this is the programme that runs my life. Every morning I go for coffee, and years later, even when I know the coffee is not good for me, it makes me jittery; I still follow the programme that I have created for myself.

This is described as limited possibilities because my possibilities are limited by my actions, memory and desire. This is an example about coffee but can easily be applied to all aspects of our lives, our behaviours, feelings, thoughts and physical habits.

My life, like many, has been steeped in perception, my software, these imprints have been there, and as I've grown, so have they. One of my earlier perceptions was that I need to work hard for a living. I had a nursery rhyme book that I used to read as a child, and I loved it.

'Monday's child is fair of face, Tuesday's child is full of grace, Wednesday's child is full of woe, Thursday's child has far to go, Friday's child is loving and giving, Saturday's child works hard for a living and the child that is born on the sabbath day is bonny and gay.'

I was born on a Saturday, and Saturday's child works hard for a living. Now, this is only a nursery rhyme. However, when your parents instil a mindset of also working hard for a living, you begin to take on the persona of one who works hard for a living. So much so that your perception, your software, turns it into a desire. In my case, if you are not flogging yourself into the ground, then you're not working hard enough. As a little girl growing up, my interpretation of working hard led me to believe that I always had to take the hard road. Taking the easy road wasn't an option, as it meant I wasn't working hard enough.

Over the years, as I grew into an adult, the software left an imprint that was compounded further by my experiences. Instead of seeing those experiences as separate, my software, my mind, linked them together. Making it impossible for the unconscious mind to understand the experiences were different.

In those moments of working hard, I never once looked up to see if the effort I was putting in was making the progress I wanted to make. When I did eventually look up, I knew immediately working hard for the sake of working hard, and pushing myself to the limits, would never give me what I longed for. Yet I perceived

I needed to work even harder because if I didn't, I wouldn't get promoted. I wouldn't have a successful business; I wouldn't have the financial rewards or a successful relationship. If I didn't fulfil this criteria, I would be a failure. This was what I thought, and this is what I created. Over time that is exactly what I attracted – everything felt like hard work, and I failed. I became my own self-fulfilling prophecy.

The memory had already been installed in my software from when I failed my A-Levels at the age of 18, when I failed to get into university, and when I failed in my first secretarial job and many jobs after that. Each time the software told me I needed to work harder. Life felt like a struggle and constant hard work. So regardless of how many hours I worked, the number of tasks I juggled and the volume of projects I cleared, I always felt I had to prove myself. This need to prove myself was born out of failure, and it played out in all aspects of my life.

It's easy to get caught up in the emotions attached to your situation, and whilst I was trying to prove myself and show I was not a failure, I was feeling completely the opposite. The more I tried, the bigger the failure I felt. I found myself feeding this perception, and that is what we do as humans – we feed our perceptions – our software. When situations such as getting overlooked for promotion, your relationship breaks down, or you don't get that pay rise, we immediately feel sorry for ourselves, and we start to blame others for the lack of our success. When in these kinds of situations, we can become angry, feel helpless and question, why me? It becomes easier to lay blame at others' feet rather than our own. This is known as being caught up in your own drama.

The drama triangle is a psychological game, and it's often a game we don't know the rules to.

The drama triangle was first described by Stephen Karpman in 1981. It is used in psychology to describe the way in which we present ourselves as 'victims,' 'persecutors,' and 'rescuers.' Although all three are roles, and none may be true to who we really are, we can all get caught up in a cycle that is hard to escape.

Once triggered, you may find you will take on a role or act out all three roles, and your ego will preside.

I had noticed my passive passenger voice was changing; it was becoming more aggressive. The tone had shifted; it now had become more persecutory. My mindset was that I would not fail. I had to prove it to myself and to everyone else. Even though my previous failings were a distant memory to others. Time had done its thing; the only problem was I hadn't let go. I was still caught up in the drama of it all. The meditation had helped me to see beyond this, but I kept pulling myself back into this place of self-persecution.

I was peeling away the layers, one by one. To get to the depths of where I needed to get to, I had to understand the emotional baggage that I was still carrying around. I wasn't sure how to approach dealing with the shame, guilt, humiliation and pain that I was still carrying for the loss of my business. I knew it was more than just that, something else needed to be addressed.

Even though my new business was thriving, I couldn't accept the success. The sense that everything would be OK felt impossible, and my software was telling me something else. When I paused and reflected, my anger reappeared. This was my ego talking, and it became my critical companion. My ego had presented a new persona. No one else was doing this to me. Only me. Without realising it, I would draw others into my drama.

I would make people feel sorry for me, and I would want people to rescue me, to prop me up emotionally and tell me I was doing great. I became the victim, and the memories of how I felt came crashing back. My immediate thought was that I didn't work hard enough; I wasn't worthy enough to be successful. All this was my software of my soul being downloaded again and replayed to me.

I wanted that validation from others, but when I received it, I didn't like it. I felt angry for the praise and recognition. I could do this on my own; I didn't need anyone to help me. Even though I'd asked for it. When others offered up suggestions and gave their advice, I got enraged. I made it clear I didn't need their help; I could do this on my own, and I knew what I was doing. I didn't stay playing the victim for long as I was angry; I blamed the recession, my ex-husband, the bank, the clients who hadn't paid their bills. But most of all, I blamed myself, and my critical companion, who was by my side, said in its familiar voice: *I told you so, you just didn't work hard enough.*

This cycle of drama can go on and on, and the emotions attached feel real, and this is what becomes imprinted. Being caught up will affect your emotions, how you see, feel and experience the world. It will affect your behaviour, and your memory will amplify it even more.

So how does it work?

When the victim mode shows up, it's usually because you are feeling overwhelmed, a need is not being met or you don't want to take accountability for your situation or how you feel. You may hear yourself saying, 'I don't know', 'I can't do this', 'I am feeling overwhelmed', 'I'm trying, but it's just not working'. You may also hear yourself say, 'I'm misunderstood or underappreciated' or

'You don't understand'. However the vibe is 'Help me, help me, help me'.

In my case, I was screaming out for help as I was drowning in my workload. My fear of failing again was overwhelming. My narrative was so strong I sucked my family members and friends into my drama.

When caught up in someone else's drama, you get triggered, and in my case, my family and friends fell into the trap of rescuing.

When we move into the rescuer mode, you will start to give advice – 'Have you considered…? Have you tried this…?' – and you will offer up solutions and sometimes take ownership of actions or tasks that don't belong to you – you may even become over supportive. Sound familiar?

The problem is when in victim mode, you don't want others to tell you what to do or even help, even though that's the vibe you're giving off. So, when support is offered, it will be rejected. This will show up in your behaviour and how you react. You won't be fully invested in what's been suggested, and you will show signs of disengagement and resistance. When this happens, you shift from the victim role into the persecutor role. You will be overt in your behaviour and will disagree openly with what has been suggested, or you will take a passive-aggressive stance. Go behind the backs of those who are trying to help and complain, moan and groan to anyone who will listen. Each time drawing more and more people into your drama.

As your drama continues, your family and friends will now also be caught up in their drama, feeling hurt and sorry for themselves as they were only trying to help you. They too will complain, this time about you. They, like you, will go round and round their drama, moving from victim to persecutor to rescuer. This game, impossible to win, leaves everyone exhausted and frustrated with how they feel. The longer we stay here it will have an impact on our emotional wellbeing. We will lose our confidence, self-belief and our self-worth.

The only way to stay out of the drama is to remain in adult ego state. We have an adult-to-adult conversation with ourselves or others. We listen to ourselves and explore how we can help ourselves. We move away from the victim role by introducing the concept of empowerment. When we do this, we move into the role of creator, meaning that we can start to accept the situation.

We draw down on the power of choice, we explore alternatives and build the capacity to solve our own problem. When this happens, the persecutor dissolves, and we become assertive, and in a constructive manner, we start to find ways to meet our needs. We take responsibility for ourselves and how we feel. When in adult ego state, you see yourself as capable of making choices and solving your own problems. Knowing that you are creative, resourceful and whole. The skill is to raise your self-awareness and learn how to stay out of your own emotional drama.

I had to deal with my ego once and for all. My critical companion was not my friend, it was my foe. I had to try to remove the emotions attached to my experiences. It was the only way to overcome what I was feeling. I needed to see it for what it was, not what I perceived it was. The emotions I was carrying around with me were those of failure and shame. I had not worked hard enough; I had let myself down. I had let others down, which brought me back to my old self-talk: *I'm not worthy. I'm not good enough.*

I started to peel away the emotion by asking myself a series of questions. Answering these questions helped me shift from my emotional state (victim) into a pragmatic one (adult). The first question I asked myself was, 'Do you want to live the rest of your life feeling like this?' No, was the answer. Then, 'What do you want to change within yourself?' and, 'How do you want to experience your life from now onwards?'

I couldn't answer the second two questions to begin with, but over time I started to retrain my brain and the only way to do that was to stop. I needed to shift my state of awareness and make more conscious choices. My first choice was that I would continue to rebuild what I had, but I would do it in a very different way – starting from now.

I would not allow my perceptions to get in the way of my truth. I would build a better relationship with the real me, not the person I perceived. I would accept myself and my capabilities and, over time, accept I was worthy. This felt like a huge milestone. I wanted to try to let go of my critical companion, the internal chatter, the negative self-talk. I have come to realise that you never get rid of your critical companion voice. But you will, over time, tame its presence. All I had to do was to learn how to live with the darker and lighter shades of my being and to pay attention to the things that really mattered.

This was not an easy task to do. I had to reprogramme my software. When trying to figure this out and tame my critical companion, I chose to go back to my breathing exercises and become present with my situation. My perception resided in my head; these were my thoughts. I needed to listen from a different place. I decided to listen only to what I knew. I stopped listening to my thoughts and my feelings, and I listened to what I knew deep inside me.

When we are caught up in our own drama, we tend to rely on what we think or what we feel; we rarely focus on what we know. There is a huge difference between what the head and heart tell us versus what we truly know deep within. Ideally, we should go there first to seek answers from our place of knowing. This is where I would describe our true sense of self resides. But we don't, as we always opt for familiarity; we are driven again by our ego wanting to keep us safe and small.

When we are seeking answers from our minds, we will always be thinking. 'I think…' will be how we start our sentences. We will over analyse and will be sucked into the narrative, the perception or the story we are telling ourselves. When we seek answers from our heart, we will be flooded with emotions, and we will start our sentences with, 'I feel…' Yet when we go to our place of knowing, we are reaching into the depth of our bellies. This is our place of knowing. This is where our true self lies and when we engage with it, we become informed. We don't need to keep going to the head or the heart; there is no need to. When you seek answers from your place of knowing, you get the truth. There will be no more perceptions, only the truth of what you know about yourself. I had been practising this for several months, and I was all over the place. I knew that there was more to my desire than the output of hours and commitment to hard work. There was something bigger at play here. I started to listen at a much deeper level beyond the head and heart, and I sunk myself into my gut. To what I knew about myself. I wanted to get out of my drama triangle.

I had to pay attention to what I knew. When I meditated on this, I found myself crying, unsure of why. I kept posing the questions I had been unable to answer: 'What do you want to change within yourself?' And: 'How do you want to experience your life from now onwards?'

I asked myself repeatedly, 'What do you want to change within yourself?' Nothing came for weeks, and then out of the blue, I heard myself say, 'My vulnerability'. I wanted this to shift. If I could change how I felt within myself, then I could hopefully move on. When acknowledging it, it felt right. I was vulnerable, and even though I'd been peeling away the layers and already come so far, I was still protecting myself – from failing, from getting hurt, from my shame. These things were keeping me vulnerable. This was hard for me to acknowledge, but in my knowing, it was my truth. Being vulnerable kept me in my drama triangle.

I'd finally got to the root cause. Instead of judging myself, I simply accepted this is where I was. The act of acknowledging it was enough for me to see a way forward. When I said it out loud, I am vulnerable, I am still lost, I am frightened of failing and I am ashamed; I found the smallest of openings in the emotional maze I'd been trapped in. I stepped out of my drama triangle.

I had made meaning. I understood that my needs were not being met, and instead of judging or criticising, I gave myself a different kind of support.

I posed myself the final question I had not yet answered: 'How do I want to experience my life from now on?'

'With compassion, self-love and kindness', was my answer.

We all have a choice, you can allow your memories to manage you or you can learn to manage your memories. Learning to manage your thoughts, rather than be managed by them is a new programme we all need to install in our software. It allows us to see the truth behind the emotion. It also stops us from storytelling, exaggerating, adding two and two together and making five. It allows us to really understand what is happening in that moment. It helps us make meaning of the experience and realise that yes, we may have experienced something similar in our past. But the experience you are experiencing now is completely new. It is happening right now, not then. We will not experience the experience the same. Why? Because we have evolved and who we are now is not who we were then.

When you allow yourself to not be led and controlled by your thoughts or memories, you step out of your drama triangle. The choices each of us makes are what differentiates one person from another. Those choices, based on past actions, create memories and then prompt future actions. The seeds of these memories and desires are stored at the level of the soul, but we can choose to plant new seeds – download a new software.

We can release ourselves from that negative software and go beyond our action, memory and desire. We can unlock ourselves from the shackles that hold us in our habitual ways of being. We can free ourselves and create space for infinite possibilities and connect with our essential nature. Our true knowing.

So, the next time you notice your perception is clouding the reality of a situation, try to make meaning of your feelings first before getting caught up in your own emotional drama and psychological game. Remember that if we don't take time to make meaning of the situation, our memory will reintroduce how we felt in the past and will, for sure, mix it with how we feel in the now.

You can choose to be in control of your memories; they do not need to control you.

Exercise

When answering the following questions, please practise compassion. Remember to speak/write your truth and take your time to determine what is your perception versus what is your reality.

Consider the following questions:

- When was the last time you got caught up in your emotional drama?

- What was the trigger point and how did you behave, what did you do, say and feel? Capture each role if you experienced them (victim, persecutor and rescuer).

- What is your typical default role?

- Does this have to be your reality?

- What perceptions are no longer serving you well?

- What is your reality? Go to what you know – not what you think or feel – what do you know?

8

CHAPTER 5

Self-limiting Beliefs

'Fear doesn't exist anywhere except in the mind.'

Dale Carnegie

Knowing you can choose to be in control of your memories, and they do not need to control you, is great, but that does not stop the emotions from creeping in. Acknowledging and accepting your truth is the starting point, but we need to go one step further before we can fully let go and move into the next phase of this journey.

As humans, we have the capacity to self-sabotage. We throw obstacles down and put roadblocks in our way, which stop us from succeeding or achieving what we really want. When you stop yourself in your tracks, you may find yourself faced with the impossible task of climbing over the hurdle, the roadblock or the obstacle that's in your way.

Some obstacles that lie in front of us are often out of our control. This is because, quite simply, we are not in control of others. The ones we are going to focus on are the obstacles we throw down ourselves. These are the ones we can control, yet we make it difficult for ourselves to get to the finish line. It is about time that we faced our self-sabotaging tendencies and our self-limiting beliefs.

I mentioned earlier that the ego has many names. So far we have discovered the passive passenger and the critical companion, and now we have the main character, the baddy, the traitor: 'Villainous Fear.'

Fear is our biggest threat. I'm introducing this to you now, halfway through our journey together, because when we're not looking, when we're making good progress and when we start to feel good, fear raises its ugly head and makes its presence known.

Fear is what causes us to stop in our tracks; it's our biggest and most threatening emotion. When fear is present, it will preside over you. Like a villain in a movie, it wants to take the lead role and prevent you from being the superhero in your own life. Fear is unpredictable; it will keep you on your toes. It will keep you second-guessing, all in aid of stopping you from making progress.

When fear is present, it will manifest into everything you do. Over time it will paralyse you and turn your thoughts against you until they become self-limiting. These self-limiting thoughts will become self-limiting beliefs. Once a seed of a self-limiting belief is planted, it will grow and grow and grow until you can't see beyond the density of the weeds.

Fear is a vital response to physical and emotional danger; if we didn't feel it, we couldn't protect ourselves from legitimate threats. But often, we fear situations that are far from life and death. This makes us hang back, deliberate, over analyse and over question for no good reason. These fears vary depending upon the situation you are faced with. When you emotionally stretch yourself by taking a potential new step, such as making a life choice, a decision about your career, where you live or your relationship, this will take you out of your comfort zone and place you right in the centre of your fear zone.

When in this space, you feel stuck and overwhelmed. Your vulnerabilities will start to come to the forefront. Self-doubt will be present, and before you know it, you will be paralysed by fear. Fear is not a place that you should reside for a long time. If we indulge in fear, we will remain frightened, scared of making the wrong choices, and remain in limbo for the rest of our lives.

Being in limbo is no good for anyone. Over time that limbo will become a state of mind and then a state of being. If you collude with fear, it will block you from living your life fully. If you are here for too long, you will start to create a new comfort zone around your fear. You will become comfortable being uncomfortable. Like me, wearing shoes that didn't fit, but each day I still put them on and walked through my life.

This is when living life in limbo will become your norm, and the longer you stay here, comfortable being uncomfortable, your confidence, self-belief and energy will be depleted. Your outlook will become negative or even cynical. You will become anxious, stressed and frustrated. All this will affect your physical, mental and emotional wellbeing. The inner conflict you will experience will affect the relationship with yourself and the one you have with others. Fear tends to make us do things that are out of character; it will make you behave in ways you never knew you were capable of. It brings a pressure, and it stops us from being in flow.

Fears are unique to you; others may share the same fear, such as fear of failure, but how you experience fear is unique. You may even be frightened of success. Whatever it is, fear will present itself; it will raise its ugly head and make itself known. It's at this point you need to know how to deal with it, how to overcome it, so you don't fall into the same behaviours or self-sabotaging traps that you have set for yourself.

Fear also has a universal trigger, and that is threat or harm. Perceived or real. The threat could be physical, emotional, or psychological. While we may have our own triggers, it is usually fear that sits underneath them – a silent assassin waiting to attack. This can be described as flight, fight, freeze or fawn response.

Let's explore this concept further.

Fight, flight and freeze are most probably familiar to you. When you encounter threat, you either resist or retaliate or simply flee. This is your body's natural reaction to danger. This response instantly causes hormonal and physiological changes in the body. You act quickly so you can protect yourself; it's a survival instinct developed from our ancient ancestors.

When in flight or fight, you are in active defence response mode, your heart rate gets faster, your breathing becomes shallow, your pain perception drops, and your hearing sharpens. All this helps you act rapidly. When in freeze mode, you simply put yourself on hold, where you protect yourself even more. It can also be called reactive immobility – you stay completely still and get ready for your next move.

When faced with a trigger, your reaction begins in your amygdala, the part of your brain responsible for perceived fear; this sends signals to the hypothalamus, which stimulates the automatic nervous system. The automatic nervous system consists of the sympathetic and parasympathetic nervous systems, and depending upon your reaction, will determine which system dominates. The sympathetic nervous system drives fight or flight, whereas the parasympathetic nervous system drives freezing.

When the automatic nervous system is triggered, our body releases adrenaline and cortisol, the stress hormone. When this happens, it will immediately have an impact on your physical body. You will see an increase in your heart rate and blood pressure. You will sweat, your breathing will be shallow and rapid, and over time, your immunity will weaken.

In modern-day living, flight, fight and freeze show up in many life situations. Slamming on the breaks when the car in front of you stops suddenly; feeling unsafe while walking down the street; getting shouted at by a passing cyclist for crossing the road and not seeing them. Most of us live our lives in a high state of alert where our nervous system is easily triggered. All this leaves us feeling fragile, exhausted and on edge. Constant high states of alert can, however, be brought on by non-threatening situations and when triggered, our responses can be described as over-reactive. Overactive responses are common in people who have experienced trauma.

When fear places its icy hand on yours, the ego is in full flow. We can easily disconnect and become untethered from ourselves. This can happen during traumatic and stressful experiences and can remain with us forever unless we do something about it. In these moments, we separate from ourselves, and the ego fights to stay small, to stay stuck, remain scared and to judge everything you do.

In my case, fear was brought on by continued trauma, from my initial bullying at school when I was eight years old, to my early twenties where I was sexually assaulted by my boss, to the dysfunctional first marriage I found myself in and to the loss of my livelihood, my home and my self-worth. Leading me to my vulnerabilities – humiliation, pain, guilt and shame. This is where the fourth response can be triggered. This is known as the fawn response. This involves immediately moving into trying to please people to avoid any conflict. This can be brought on by early childhood trauma, caused by verbal, physical or sexual abuse. By the time I was 22 years old I had experienced all of these – verbal, physical and sexual abuse.

In my early twenties, I wanted to escape my hometown, I was sick of being bullied and called names, and I had lost my faith in those I thought I could trust. Life at home was unfulfilling. I'd had a series of secretarial jobs as I didn't secure the right grades to get into university. My sense of loss and grief for a life I dreamed of was overwhelming. Out of sheer luck, I managed to get a job as a holiday representative in Greece. This was my ticket to something new and a fresh start. I didn't realise I was jumping from the frying pan into the fire. My naivety or sheer ignorance landed me front and centre of danger. Not perceived danger, but real danger.

When I arrived, I was met by my boss and his assistant who were to initiate me to life in Greece. This consisted of drinking – a lot, partying with guests, dancing on bars and running the weekly monster bar crawl. This also included being verbally abused by my boss in front of the holidaymakers, being ridiculed and sexually exploited to pull in the punters. One night he decided to take the abuse one step further. I woke up to the smell of stale alcohol, his body weight on top of me, heavy panting, one heavy-set hand over my mouth, the other in a place it shouldn't have been. My fear took hold of me. Freezing first, I didn't know what to do; this was soon followed by fight as I kicked and bit my way out of his grip. I literally flew home. I ran away and got as far away from the situation as I could. But the trauma of it stayed with me. Instead of talking about it and getting the support I needed, I buried it deep in the hope I would forget. But the imprint was far greater than I could have imagined, and the shame and humiliation that surfaced were unsurmountable.

I didn't realise then what impact my past would have on who I would be in my future. From being eight years old when my first bullying trauma was experienced, I had become a people pleaser. I said and did what I needed to, to fit in. When I was 16, I changed my nose in the hope that my appearance would please others so I could be liked and fit in. By the time I moved into my full adulthood, after my experience in Greece, I pre-emptively attempted to appease everyone. I ignored my own personal feelings and desires and did anything and everything to prevent myself from being abused.

This narrative fuelled my fear even further. My fear had turned into a self-limiting belief, and this belief went with me wherever I went. I carried this with me for years; it weighed heavy. Over the years, my frustration, anger and resentment became my norm, and the only way to deal with it was to ignore it or lash out when I was feeling sorry for myself. Fear made me behave in ways I did not like. I didn't fully recognise how I was behaving because I was trying so hard not to get hurt. I didn't know who I was; my identity changed as I moved through my life. At times it was difficult to identify how I really felt because I always looked to others to tell me how to feel, in my relationships or in the situation. At the first sight of conflict, I would run away, literally move towns or cities, or if I stayed, I would appease the person or the situation. I ignored my own beliefs, thoughts, truths and instead, I accepted those of the people around me.

I would find it difficult to give my true opinion – I didn't believe my thoughts or opinions mattered. I lacked boundaries in my relationships, and over time, I would give everything to a friendship or an intimate relationship. I gave away my independence, judgment and I allowed myself to be taken advantage of. This showed up everywhere, and I carried this into my first marriage and then into my first business. People took advantage of me. I allowed that to happen. I let them do that to me. I found saying no to be the most problematic thing. I was frightened of letting people down, what they would think of me and would they still like me. I gave away all my personal power because I was frightened.

This pattern of behaviour had been a regular occurrence. I look back on these experiences as missed opportunities to live my life on my terms. When my world had turned upside down, I didn't want to take this with me. I wanted to be me. The narrative had been so strong that the story I believed to be true became true. Who you are is what you believe, and what you believe determines what you do, the choices you make and how you make them.

I allowed fear to be the dominant character in my story. The more I colluded and fed my fear, the bigger the villain became. He towered over me for years, engulfing me; trapped and unable to move, I was paralysed by it. Stopping me from having the life I longed for.

I had a firm belief that a little girl from a small market town would never be good enough, so instead of getting rejected or hurt, I chose to keep myself safe. I believed it, and it became my story.

The day of reckoning came for me when I finally made the decision to tame the voice of villainous fear in the hope that I could let it go for good.

I hadn't, until it all came crumbling down, managed to put the pieces of my jigsaw together. To see the full picture. As each experience made its mark, I compartmentalised them, and when packed away in their boxes, the lid firmly on – I moved on. I didn't stop to understand, to reflect or even to seek help. I pushed what happened down in the hope they would not reveal themselves to me again.

I suppose, like most trauma, big or small, if you push it down, don't deal with it at the time, it will return. Brought on by the trigger of fear, you become a prisoner, held hostage by your limiting beliefs.

I mentioned at the beginning of the book I chose to swim, not sink. I chose to survive. I eventually paid off the debt, but my approach to work remained the same. The challenge I had with the fawn mode was that it would still show up years after my wake-up call. I never considered myself successful. I never gave myself praise for what I had accomplished. I found myself working harder, still flogging myself into the ground. I couldn't understand why. I didn't need to follow that programme anymore. But I still harboured my traumas. The memories were strong, and when the mind was not busy with working, they came through. I thought they'd been buried, but as I had started to peel away the layers, to get closer to who I was, the more I remembered. The more I remembered, the more painful the memory was. I didn't tell anyone about this, not because I didn't want to speak my truth and express how I was feeling; it was because I didn't know what to do with it. I needed to figure it out first before I burdened anyone else with it.

The memories that had emotion attached to them had been traumatic for me, and they influenced how I showed up in the world. I would hear myself mutter about feeling small, weak, not good enough. I'd call myself stupid and undermine myself – a lot.

I found myself reacting rather than responding. I knew I should rely upon my sense of knowing, not my head or heart, but the memories that were presenting were still controlling me rather than me controlling them.

After the debt, there was a gaping hole that needed to be filled, and that's when all of my past memories flooded in. I cut my way through the density of the weeds I'd allowed to grow. It felt like a mammoth task, and I kept falling into the self-sabotaging traps that I had laid out for myself.

My new focus was to be free from my past, and with grit and determination, I took off each lid and carefully unpacked my beliefs about me. When I started to recall the experiences and remember the feelings, I could start to see the very fine dotted line that linked the experience to the pattern that influenced my behaviour. I was full of shame, humiliation, guilt and pain. The fear of being free from this kept me from celebrating my success and achievements. From feeling fully content and fulfilled. The hard work had paid off, but I couldn't let go of those feelings. If I kept harbouring these experiences and did not deal with them in the way that honoured them, in the stark daylight, their ugliness would always remain. I would never be able to come home to my true self if I did not deal with my past.

I reset my focus and posed a new question: 'How can I let go of my past?'

I was on the scenic route now, and I knew this destination would not be enjoyable, but equally, I needed to stop off, take a good look around. I needed to fully let go of the things still ruminating within me. The relationship I had built with my past experiences were no longer serving me well. I wanted to move on and stand at the top of the mountain I'd climbed and appreciate the view.

I had to get out of the holding pattern villainous fear had got me locked into. I needed to find a way through my roadblock. Instead of being frightened, I needed to lean in once again. I needed to reframe my past experiences and learn to build a new relationship with my past. One that didn't have the drama, the blame, me as the victim or the persecutor.

Reframing is a powerful way of looking at things through fresh eyes. Going beyond the drama, the roles and the words. To see love instead of fear. If I chose love instead of fear, it might help me remove the roadblocks and obstacles I had in front of me. So, I started to reframe.

When you can learn to do this for yourself, you will learn to honour the whole of you, including the parts that have been hidden or locked away. I wanted to remove the fear and write my villain out of the script. I knew I could tame my ego and learn to manage it. I had to go beyond ego-based awareness and give myself some compassion. As I was clearing out a drawer in my office, I found the fluorescent star I'd written on at the end of my original coach training programme. The course that helped me transition into becoming a coach. Sixteen years previously, I'd written, 'I have learned to love me for being me.'

A gentle reminder from the universe and my catalyst for true change. One that would deepen my acceptance, find true appreciation, give myself the right level of affection and be aware of what I needed to pay attention to.

The word forgiveness floated in; I needed to forgive myself and accept that what happened in my past was not my fault. I did not invite those experiences into my life. I did not ask for them. But I could give myself compassion for them, and I could forgive the child, the teenager and the woman who had experienced them. I had already given myself the incredible gift of choice – I had free will. I didn't need to survive anymore; I was doing more than surviving. I was on the cusp of thriving.

I posed the following questions to help me reframe how I felt about myself, to move beyond my limiting beliefs so I could embrace my future.

- *What do I accept?* I accepted the scars of my past; instead of covering them up, I sat down and shared them with my immediate family. I accepted that I was whole; I no longer needed to be vulnerable and carry my shame.

- *What do I appreciate?* I accepted deeply that this was where I was meant to be, where I was supposed to be in my life. I accepted it was OK to be where I was. I appreciated my journey would be one I didn't have to walk alone. The path I would walk would take me to where I needed to get to. I would continue to grow and learn. I appreciated I could be free of all the things I'd buried.

- *What affection do I need?* I decided that I wanted to give myself the gift of gratitude; that was the affection I needed. Instead of fighting against my past, the pressure of working hard and the people who'd hurt me, I embraced it all and became thankful for it. Without those experiences, who would I be? I wouldn't be the person I had become. I was beginning to like who I was, and this would allow me to be me.

- *What did I need to pay attention to?* I decided that I would live my life only in the present, not focus on the past and hold grudges or be fearful of the future. My attention would be in the present moment. I would be fully in the here and the now.

Once I had written these down and said them out loud, a huge weight lifted. The emotions that had been buried came to the surface, and instead of burying them back down again, I allowed them to wash over me. I didn't judge myself for this; instead, I tuned into how I felt, and for the first time ever in my life, I remained true to those feelings.

Moving beyond your limiting beliefs and beyond villainous fear is easier said than done because, like any villain, fear does not want to be written out of the script; it wants to remain in the leading role. But to save yourself and be the hero in your own story, you need to believe you can do it and invite love in. Like any hero or heroine's journey – love always conquers fear.

When I did this, I learned I could walk freely towards the horizon, knowing that I didn't need to feel fear in my life any longer. My new story had optimism and infinite possibilities. I had reframed how I viewed my world and how I viewed myself.

I learned that everything I wanted was on the other side of my fear.

Exercise

Consider the following questions:

- What roadblocks/obstacles do you put in your own way?
- What limiting beliefs are driving your behaviour?
- What stops you from facing your fears?

Once you have the clarity you need like I did, try the reframing exercise and answer the following questions:

- What do I accept?
- What do I appreciate?
- What affection do I need?
- What do I need to pay attention to?

After that, once the words have settled on the page, and within you, I would like you to read your answers out loud so the universe can hear you. By doing this, you are setting your intention, and it's important to call forth the Law of Attraction. We will be exploring more of this later in the book.

8

CHAPTER 6

Let Go To Let Come

'In the process of letting go, you will lose many things from the past, but you will find yourself.'

Deepak Chopra

When going on any journey, it's important you take with you what you need and only what you need. But most of us always pack more, always carry more than we need – just in case. I've always had a habit of stuffing my suitcase to the full leaving no room for anything else.

Mindset encourages us to carry more than we need: 'I might need this – I will bring this just in case.' Our luggage bursting to the seams, backpacks so heavy, we end up with sore shoulders, stiff necks and back pain.

Carrying a heavy load is what most of us do all of our lives. That heavy load becomes familiar. It's the emotional baggage that no longer serves us, but we hold on to it just in case. The 'just in case' mindset is something we may not always be conscious of. When we *are* conscious of it, our dreaded villain may present itself again, and fear will be fuelled through our body and mind. When we're not conscious of it, we carry on, not aware that life could be different. But it can be different if only you can learn to fully let go. This is the final step of looking inward. Once we do this, we can then move forward into the next phase of our journey together.

So far, we have been unlocking past conditioning, the labels and roles we have attached ourselves to. We have learned to quieten the mind, understand what being true to ourselves looks and feels like, and we have reframed our limiting beliefs and fears. But to truly move on, we have to release the past so we can enter our future.

In this chapter we will be focusing on letting go to let come. This concept was created by Otto Scharmer, we are using his philosophy to help us in this next stage of our journey.

If you can fully master letting go of your past, those things that are not working for you any longer, you will be able to move forward freely, with a fresh energy and a new purpose. There will be nothing pulling you back, and you will free yourself of old patterns of living. As you move closer to coming home to your true self, you need to create some space within you so you can truly create the life you want to live.

For you to get to where you belong, you must acknowledge the person you once were. The person who played roles, the person who held themselves in patterns of behaviour, must be let go of, so the truest version of yourself can fully emerge.

Like any transformation, something needs to end for something new or refined to emerge. Like the caterpillar in its cocoon, it lets go and succumbs to its full transformation, and after a period of time, a butterfly emerges.

When I moved beyond my fear and limiting beliefs, I thought I had mastered everything, life was going to be amazing, and it was. But as we know, the universe always has a way of testing you. Checking that the lesson that was taught had been fully mastered. I had learned to tame my fear and my ego, but as I stepped out into my new world, I started to notice some cracks appear. Hairline cracks, but ones I did not want to deepen or widen.

My debt was paid off, my new business was going great, opportunities were presenting themselves and life was good. My son was happy, I had fallen in love again, and as a new family, we had started to create a lovely home and life for ourselves. I was happy. But I was also restless. Something was still hovering, and I couldn't quite fathom what.

I had accepted my past and appreciated where I was in my journey, and I knew if I continued to give myself love and compassion, then I would find my way back home to my true self. What became apparent was that I hadn't truly let go of it all. I was still carrying a heavy load; my backpack still held some remains of my past.

Our past is important to us; without the past we would not be here today and it makes us who we are. Accepting it and appreciating it for what it has given us, is important. But it doesn't mean that we have to continue to carry it around with us for the rest of our lives. We have the choice to let some or all of it go.

Let's explore this concept further. Imagine you are carrying a backpack around with you every day; it's heavy, it's full of all the emotional baggage from your past. Some of that baggage will be things you want to keep and take with you as you emerge into your future, and there will be some baggage you want to unpack, offload and leave behind. If you hold onto the baggage, continue to take all of it with you, there will be no room for anything new. As we walk towards the future, we must have space within so we can experience new things, meet new people and explore what life has to offer us. But when we are chock-a-block, full to the brim, there just isn't any room for anything new to emerge. We will, over time, go back to our old ways of feeling, being and doing as the backpack will weigh heavy, and we will, over time, succumb once again to who we were, not to who we are meant to become.

Letting go is hard to do. We can use this concept and apply it to everything in our life; for example, if you are in a toxic relationship with a friend or partner, you know you need to let it go, but it keeps you in that holding pattern. You do the same thing day in day out; your backpack is full to the brim. You can't give any more to the relationship. No matter how hard you have tried to make it work, you are exhausted, tired and heavy with the strain. You want to try new things, meet new people, but you can't. Why? Because your backpack has no room for anything new. To create space, you need to let go for something different or new to appear.

Or perhaps you are trapped in a cycle at work, you get paid a great salary and have great benefits, but you are deeply unsatisfied with your work. It brings no pleasure or joy. Your days drag on and on and on. Over time you notice your confidence dwindle, and your energy and drive disappear. But every day, you mindlessly get ready for work, put on the same suit and do the same again. Your backpack weighing heavy full of self-doubt, lack of confidence and belief that you would never get a job anywhere else. No one would employ you on the same salary with the same benefits. You start to apply for jobs, but you never get them. You notice other people in your department moving on, getting new jobs, but you can't seem to secure something new. Why? Because your self-doubt, your lack of job satisfaction and lack of confidence are stopping anything new coming to you. You are full up.

You may even want to improve your fitness, you are a little overweight and definitely out of shape, you have been talking to your friends about getting fit for years, but nothing seems to change. You look at your schedule and try to rearrange your daily activities to get to the gym or go out for a run, but your life keeps taking over. You are busy with the kids, balancing work, the household and chores. There simply is no time for you. You watch your neighbours go out for their daily runs; you see your work colleagues going to the gym, but you simply can't find the time. Why? Because you are doing the same thing, and you're at capacity. You have no space for yourself as you are full doing things for others.

But what happens when you tip your backpack upside down and let all its contents spill out onto the floor? You empty every item out, and you lay it all out on the floor. Simple, you get to see what you're carrying around with you, and more importantly, you get the chance to decide if you want to throw some stuff away or repack any of it.

This is a very important lesson to learn. We don't have to carry around our past, our baggage forever; we can simply choose what we want to leave behind and what we want to take with us. Although the idea of this sounds simple, we all know the reality of this. It's not that easy to do. This is our final test – to free ourselves of those things that are no longer serving us well so we can embrace our future with space for new things to emerge. We must let go, to let come.

So how do we do this?

Most want the easiest and quickest route, but that won't sustain the transformational change that needs to take place. For true transformation to take place, we must make sure villainous fear, the critical companion, the passive passenger and a voice of the ego we have not yet met – cynicism – don't get in our way. Being cynical is something we have all experienced at times throughout our lives. We will have experienced others being cynical. This is not a good or healthy trait to have. It will have a negative impact on how you think and how you feel, and it will keep your mind closed. With this also comes suspicion and that all or nothing thinking – even at times maybe catastrophising. When your cynical friend appears, it is trying to keep your desires, needs and wants at bay. Instead, it will make you think the worst, and you will have a hard time seeing the good in things.

You may be reading this book, and at times, your cynical friend may appear and start to plant seeds of doubt. If that has happened or happens moving beyond this point – it's OK as it's part of the process – part of the journey that will lead you home. It's difficult to make the transition from closed-minded to open-minded. If you have been following the exercises at the end of each chapter, I have been gently opening your mind. You, of course, have had free will to do these exercises or not, yet each chapter has been inviting you to take a step closer to who you really are.

All I ask as we embark on this next step is for you to be open to the three things you must master. To be able to empty your backpack and repack only what you want to take with you, you need to do three things.

1. Keep an open mind

2. Keep an open heart

3. Have open will

All three must be open at the same time – your mind, heart and will. Here lies the challenge. There must be an alignment of all three open at the same time for them to remain open. Let me share more about this.

You could have an open mind, yet, as I have shared, if villainous fear is present, then your heart won't be free to open. Your ego will be protecting it. If you have an open heart – you are longing to make that change, but if your critical companion is hanging around, then your mind will close itself down. If both mind and heart are closed, you will never have open will.

If you can imagine a golden thread that runs from the crown of your head to the soles of your feet, and when aligned, that thread connects head, heart and will. But when not aligned, we will find that only parts of us are open. That's when we can become disconnected. When this happens, we need to reverse back into ourselves. Like a car reversing into a parking space, we need to do that within ourselves, to get back into position to become fully aligned.

I found that my mind had started to open, so had my heart along with my will, yet they were not always aligned. I'd been meditating for a couple of years, and I decided to learn how to teach it. I'd also trained to become an Ayurveda teacher and a reiki healer. Yet, at times, I found myself unable to remain fully open – my mind, heart and will.

It had taken me seven years to pay off the debt, and as I was about to marry for the second time, I did not want to take the past with me, the bits that were not serving me well. I needed to do something more permanent that would help me release me from the shackles of my past.

I needed to fully release the remains of my backpack. I knew if I kept hold of them, they would become even more toxic. The time was now to make the transition from my past, so I could walk towards my future. I was nervous and excited at the same time; the ripples of my trepidation moved through my body. Instead of repressing it, I fully invited it in and gave myself permission to empty my backpack. I wanted to be fully aligned, to make sure that as I moved forward, I would keep an open mind, I would have an open heart, and my will would remain open. If I could align my mind, my heart and will, I would be able to fully let go of the past and live in the present. My anger would be no longer relevant, and my shame, humiliation, pain and guilt would be resolved once and for all. It would be the aligning of all three at the same time that would allow my full transformation to take place.

So how do you align your mind, heart and will?

An open mind is where you suspend judgment of self and others. It's about not restricting your thinking in any way, so it holds you back. It's about seeing with fresh eyes. Meaning you are receptive and open to explore and understand in its entirety rather than only listening from a place of past knowledge. Open mind is about giving yourself permission to see things from new angles, new perspectives, not just focusing on what you're familiar with. Instead, you need to listen with curiosity about the possibilities that are open to you. Give yourself permission to suspend judgment and ask your cynical friend to pipe down.

When here, you will find acceptance in yourself; *this is where I am, this is where I am meant to be.* Once the mind is open it needs to always remain open. When open, you will be open to experiencing new things, open to letting go of those things you no longer need. When here, your mind can be reflective and alert, meaning it can expand fully to be receptive to all the new experiences entering your world.

Staying open requires a commitment and will take practice, but the more you allow your mind to stay open, the more you will cultivate a deeper acceptance of what is.

When your mind is open, you will notice there will be no inner chatter; you will have clarity of thoughts and clarity in your decision-making.

Once the mind is open, the next step is to unlock your heart.

When you introduce an open heart, the feelings and emotions that go with that immediately feel different. We become more aware of our emotional connection. This awareness raises our own self-understanding, and our heart starts to trust. We know how we feel. This is when our vision of who we are, what we're meant to be doing and how we're meant to be living shifts into full technicolour. The infinite possibilities of what is possible become fully in focus. We know how it feels deep, deep within our heart.

Having an open heart means that you have a strong belief in your abilities; you are kind to yourself and others. You are open to being vulnerable. Instead of seeing vulnerability as weakness, you embrace it as your biggest superpower. This allows you to become fully present, physically and emotionally. When you do open your heart, the experiences you have will burn bright within. You will experience compassion, kindness, forgiveness, warmth, generosity and gratitude. With an open heart comes a sense of peace within.

When your heart is open, you will feel easy within yourself. You will find the courage to tell yourself that you love yourself. When you do this, you immediately have a deeper connection, and love is present all the time.

The final unlocking that needs to take place is your will; this can be argued as the most critical to the success of this journey you're on. Having an open will means there is a readiness and a willingness that you can't ignore. You are opening up to emergence – infinite possibilities. Open will is the magic you have inside you; it's where your true self resides, your sense of self, the person who you really are. When aligned, you can connect with your sense of knowing but in a much deeper way than you have before. You will connect with the road map that will bring you home to your true self.

When fully aligned and open, you will take a mindful approach to your life, and, in that moment, you let go of your past and welcome in your present. You assign yourself one task only and that is to remain a compassionate observer of self. When you do this, you have unlocked your mind, heart and will. Your golden thread from the crown of your head to the soles of your feet is aligned. You will be centred, grounded and feel whole.

If we go back to that statement, you are born as perfection then you don't have to do anything more than remain aligned and have an open mind, an open heart and have open will. By staying aligned, you have connected to 'Source.' What comes after that is a natural release of all those things that no longer serve you well. By doing this, you create space within; you expand your awareness and sense of knowing in being.

When I was fully aligned, I decided to write a letter to my past. I felt compelled to release myself, give myself permission to move on, and in this process, I let go, to let come.

Dear Past,

I want to thank you for being in my life; you have brought me challenges that I didn't want or ask for. You have hurt me and brought me pain. I no longer want you in my life. My past experiences have made me who I am, I have learned from them, but the feelings of shame, humiliation, guilt and pain do not work for me any longer. Like a badge of honour, I have worn them, but they have not honoured me in the way I believe I should be honoured. I have been angry for a long time; I have been critical of myself and others for too long. I have held myself in fear of further humiliation and pain. I have stopped myself from fully participating in my life; through my childhood, my adolescence and womanhood. I want to be released from your grip. I am letting go of the shame I have felt, the humiliation I have held onto and my guilt of not feeling worthy or good enough. I am grateful for the experiences you have given me, but it's time to bid each other farewell. I no longer need you. Thank you and goodbye humiliation, thank you and goodbye guilt and thank you and goodbye shame. There is no place anymore for you within me, and I choose to release you, to let you go, so I can be free.

I am honouring me, the whole of me.

Farewell, Gillian

I folded the letter in half, went outside and burnt it. As the wind blew the ashes away, I knew it was time. I watched the ashes until they no longer existed. Looking out to the hills, I asked the universe for love, compassion and light to fill the empty rucksack. I invited them in. I was open and receptive to what would come next. I had no expectation. I'd forgiven myself and let go of what was not serving me. I was enough, and I no longer needed to prove that to anyone.

I had created space within, and I had the capacity to set my intentions, and when I did this, my intentions crystallised. I made a commitment to myself to focus my attention on my intention and I allowed the emergence of my future to unfold. My intention was and still is to live in the present, to trust I am exactly where I am meant to be. What has happened in the past and what will happen in my future is what I am meant to experience. I am meant to learn from all my experiences. My intention is to be content with myself just the way I am. Who I am and what I want are fully aligned. My life map has been rediscovered. I am connected to my inner compass that now has the coordinates to guide me back home.

I believed that if I let go, I would end up with nothing, but life revealed just the opposite. Letting go to let come is the real path to freedom, the path that will walk you back home to your true self.

As we come to the halfway point of our journey together, I want to remind you that you, too, can make this transition. You can, at any point, turn over the page and enter a new chapter. You can develop a new narrative, one that will allow you to make choices on what you want to accomplish in your life. You can remove any obstacle in your way. The road ahead can be clear. When you start making different choices, you will stop worrying about the what ifs and focus on what you have to gain. All you need to do is open your mind, open your heart and have open will.

Exercise

Consider the following questions:

- What do you need to do within yourself to open your mind?

- What needs to happen to open your heart?

- What do you need to shift within to open your will?

- What can you do to align all three?

I invite you to write a letter to something you want to release yourself from. Those things that will allow you to have an open mind, open heart and open will. What do you want to let go of, so you can let new things come?

Start your letter with:

Dear (name what it is you want to release yourself from),

I want to thank you for being in my life...

And finish with...

Thank you and goodbye. There is no place anymore for you within me, and I choose to release you, to let you go, so I can be free of your conditioning.

I am honouring me, my soul and my purpose.

Farewell, (name)

8

CHAPTER 7

Living With Joy

'Joy does not simply happen to us. We have to choose joy and keep choosing it every day.'

Henri Nouwen

You have created more space in your backpack, and it should now feel lighter. This doesn't mean we have to cram it full again. Instead, we can expand that space – the space you have created within. Space is good. Humans have cultivated the need to be busy – if you're busy, you're going places, so most don't like having space as they don't know what to do with it.

You may be someone who doesn't like spending time on your own, you may feel you need to pack your calendar with things to do, but it's essential you leave some space for you. I've had clients over the years who can't live without being in a relationship; when one finishes, they immediately jump into another. Leaving no space to breathe and to figure out what they want and what they don't want. Others have been anxious at the thought of having nothing scheduled, and others do not know what to do when in their own company. But when you move on, let go or make changes to your life, you must leave the space for something new to come in. It's the same with clearing out your backpack. The best way to deal with this is to welcome the new in. Accept it will be quiet at times, and you will have time on your hands. Your head won't be as full, and you won't feel as heavy. You will have a renewed energy but nothing yet to use it on.

Time on your hands is a good thing. Time gives you a moment to pause, to re-establish, to reconnect with what you really want. This is an opportunity for us to slow down and take a moment – a well-deserved moment to breathe.

Alongside being born as perfection, we are also born to have a life filled with joy. Living our life connected to our passions. We have spent a lot of time looking inwards, and now we can shift the focus and start to look outwards. Reconnecting with the things that bring us joy. We can only do this when we have created some space within. We need to have room to explore and try out different and new experiences. I'm hoping by this stage you have figured out who you are because now we need to focus on what you want in your life.

What gives you joy? What makes you happy? What makes you laugh?

It's important at this stage of our journey together that we take a deeper look at what you want in your life. I was asked several years ago what I would do if I could do anything.

I now ask you the same question: what would *you* do if you could do anything?

What would you love to do? What brings you the most joy? We all have passions, and we can all create joy in our lives, and when we choose to incorporate these two things into our lives, our life has more purpose and meaning.

Passion can be anything, from something you love doing to something that intrigues you or motivates you. Passion can be something you believe in, something that can make a difference to the world around you. With passion in your life, you will laugh more, have more fun, and a lightness within you will grow.

Looking back to your childhood, there would have been times where you were passionate and experienced sheer joy. Riding your bike hands-free. Getting caught in the rain. Running for no reason and playing for hours immersed in something that's only purpose was to bring you joy.

As we move into adulthood, we can feel overwhelmed with our responsibilities. We hear ourselves say we are time-poor. Often, we are, but regardless of how busy we all are, we should find time to connect with what brings us joy. To experience joy and find an interest outside our core responsibilities is available to us all. It's only our mind that will say we can't, and once we fall into that trap, we are back with our critical companion, passive passenger and our cynical friend. Our motivation for doing anything outside of what we think we should be doing will cease.

Living with joy is a huge part of being human. If you give yourself permission to do so, you can find a deep sense of fulfilment and contentment. When you add this into your life, you will live and breathe it; you'll light up. You'll feel energised and enthusiastic, and these emotional states will lead to more joy.

Emotional wellbeing is one of the fundamental pillars of health. Joy sits right in the centre of building a healthy life. However, most of us confuse joy for happiness, and there is a distinct difference between them. Joy is living in the present. Being in the moment. And it can stay with us because it is something we draw upon from deep within. Whereas happiness is temporary. It is transient. When happiness is present, it is larger than life, it feels good, but it can also be fickle. It can be present one moment and gone in the next. True joy is constant. Joy is a limitless transformative reservoir waiting to be tapped into. It requires us to surrender, allow it to wash over us and be present. Joy can also bring meaning to life. Joy is an inner feeling of true connection, meaning and purpose. However, we do need both in our lives – joy and those moments of happiness, regardless of how transient they are.

We have spent a lot of time exploring when our needs are not being met, and it's about time we got those needs met. Connecting with what brings us joy is our next step. To do this, we have to go back to what we love doing, regardless of our responsibilities. When you reconnect with what you love, what brings you joy, the feelings you experience will filter through to all areas of your life. When living within your passions, you live life open to new opportunities. Your inspiration will be fuelled by curiosity, and your creativity is driven by your desire to learn and experience more.

Life was not created for it to be difficult; life is a gift. Living and having fun is another remedy to finding true fulfilment. We need to embrace it even when life is a little unpredictable at times. When living in passion, you go beyond your personal enthusiasm; it penetrates all parts of your life, including love. You love fully and deeply with passion. You connect more deeply and can express a deeper and more passionate love to those around you.

When you're inspired by your passions, others will be too. It will spur your friends, co-workers and family members to feel better about their own lives and themselves. Living in your passion is contagious, and it will bring you joy.

Passion is the human equivalent of fuel that powers your car. Passion powers a lifetime of dreams, and it is an energy source for living an inspired life that is driven by purposeful action. Passion will fuel your vision for your life. It will help you tap into your core strengths, values, talents and interests. With it, you can overcome life's challenges and solve any problem thrown at you. Why? Because when experiencing joy, you are resourceful and creative.

This is where the fun comes in; passion is born from experiences, by trying new things and broadening your horizons, thinking beyond what you already know, appreciating; the possibilities for you are infinite and within your reach.

Money follows passion, and yet I see most people chasing the money first and wondering why they make very little progress. When cultivating your passions, focus on the experience of living them, not what you will get in return. When you establish what you want in your life and choose to live a life with passion, you shift into being. You don't need to force yourself into being passionate; you just become it. With passion comes joy, and life becomes more satisfying and easier. Simply because you are doing what you love doing. Living your life in the way you want to.

Your passion will propel you forward. You can see clearly beyond the current reality, and you are invited to get a glimpse of a positive and inspiring future. Passion and joy can be described as a state of mind, but for me, it's a state of being, yes, your mindset does change, but when you stop thinking about what you're doing and just be it, your life is transformed as a result. And so will the lives of those around. You will be joy, and with that, you will bring joy to others.

When you become all consumed in your responsibilities like I did, I lost my passions. Even my job, which I loved, felt like a chore. Joy was a word I'd never used. I'd gone to the gym because that was a necessity. That's all I did outside my family and work life. But was I joyful about hammering the treadmill at 6am every day? When I was asked what I wanted I didn't know. After I had let go, I didn't know what I wanted to come. I had space and time now, but I had no idea what I wanted. All I kept saying was, 'I don't know. I don't know.'

The *I don't know* answer is an interesting one because the reality is that we all have the answers inside. Sometimes we don't know where to look, and other times we choose not to look. In my case, I just didn't know where to look.

I sat for hours with a blank piece of paper and coloured pens at the ready for when inspiration hit, bemused by my rigour at trying to find what would bring me joy. The white paper remained blank. I had no hobbies. I had my exercise and meditation, but beyond that, I'd not invested my time in anything else apart from work and the debt. I asked myself again. Nothing. I reasoned that my passions could be something I believed in, something that could make a difference to the world around me. In many ways, my work was doing some of that, but there was something else that was calling me: a deep longing for joy.

I looked back to my childhood, to the times where I experienced sheer joy. Riding my bike, playing for hours, dancing in my bedroom, singing into my hairbrush, acting, reading books, making clothes, taking photographs, creating art, writing plays and short stories. It all came flooding back; I had forgotten this side to myself. It was as though I'd fallen out with my lighter self. I didn't know who that was anymore.

I loved riding my bike. I got my first bike when I was four years old and loved it then. When the stabilisers came off, I truly felt I could fly – being able to pick up traction, go fast or slow whenever I wanted. That sense of joy was instilled then and was the same when I was a teenager. I would head off on my own and cycle into the countryside close to my home. It brought me so much joy, the opportunity to escape what was going on around me. I loved the sense of freedom it gave me, the sheer joy of the wind blowing against my face. I would let my feet free of the pedals and allow my legs to stretch out, freewheeling down the hills. I still feel the same way now.

I wanted to reconnect with this side of me; it was part of me, but as I continued to stare at the blank piece of paper, I was lost for words, ideas and all the suggestions I ran through my mind were stopped. I couldn't do that. No, that won't work, and so the inner chatter continued. Frustrated with myself, I took my blank sheets of paper and coloured pens back into the spare bedroom and threw them and myself on the bed face down.

My sense of responsibility overwhelmed me, and I could hear myself say I don't have the time, and I belittled my longing. What was wrong with me? There had to be something I could do just for fun. I gave up for the night, but when I woke, the feeling was still there.

My logic kicked in; regardless of how busy I was, I could find some time to have some fun, experience joy and find an interest outside my core responsibilities. I didn't want my mind to say, *you can't do this, you're too busy*, as I'd fall back into that trap, and my motivation for doing anything outside of work would cease. Instead of forcing it, I decided to invite it in, so when I asked in my meditation practice, what do I want? I saw myself as a little girl, wearing a yellow dress; she was holding my hand and pulling me towards something, smiling and giggling, 'come on, come on,' pulling on my hand. My hair cut in a bob, my fringe framing my face. I was so happy, so enthusiastic and full of eagerness.

Simplicity appeared. It didn't have to be some expensive new hobby; I could do things that came naturally to me and things that were easy to access. What I really wanted to do was laugh and have fun and to do something for the sheer pleasure of it. I wanted to feel happy, enthusiastic and full of eagerness. The vision of me as a child had given me hope, and I followed that feeling. In my vision, I was giggling. I couldn't remember the last time I had laughed.

Laughter is another way for us to connect with the joyous self. It's strong medicine. Research has proven that laughter strengthens your immune system, boosts mood, diminishes pain and protects you from the damaging effects of stress. This is what I needed; I wanted to bring my mind and body back into balance.

As children, we laugh hundreds of times a day, but as adults, we tend to make life more serious, and our laughter is infrequent. Nothing works faster or more dependably to bring your mind and body back into balance than a good laugh. Humour lightens your burdens, inspires hope; it reconnects you to you but also connects you to others. Humour and laughter keep you grounded, focused and alert, and any frustration you may be harbouring will be released.

I was reminded again that joy did not need to be an expensive new hobby. I went back to what I knew; the easiest way for me to figure out what I wanted was to write a list of all the things I'd enjoyed over my life. That list was long, and it kept growing. I allowed myself the time to create a list of everything. I started to remember the things I loved doing, and I began to feel excited. I'd forgotten about the fun and light-hearted Gillian, the one who giggled lots, the one that had a great sense of humour and the one who loved trying new things and experiencing something different. The one who was unapologetic for practical jokes, doing silly things, laughing when others couldn't see the funny side. This is what I wanted for myself.

Music had brought me so much joy when younger, so did dancing. I loved the theatre and the arts, I loved photography and reading, though I couldn't remember the last time I'd read a book for sheer pleasure. My list was quite long, and I certainly couldn't do everything on the list all at once. So, I decided to break it down into small manageable chunks. Baby steps I called them, and it worked.

1. Listen to music every day

2. Dance around the house when no one is looking

3. Join a photography night class and take pictures

4. Go to a gig, and with your eyes closed, get lost in the music

5. Browse in a book shop, take your time and buy a novel

6. Get cosy on the sofa and read the book with a cup of tea

7. Draw anything with fat crayons

These were simple pleasures I'd not done for over 18 years, and before I knew it, I'd found my passion again for music, for dancing, for taking photos, for drawing. Regardless of my talents or not in these areas, I applied myself like I had nothing to lose and over time came the feeling of contentment. I found I loved listening to music. I played music when cleaning, when making dinner, when I got home from work, and over time, I realised that music was a key factor in helping me to relax. If I'd had a hard day, I'd turn the volume up high and would lie on the floor in the living room, allowing the music to wash over me. By the time my favourite song had finished, I was calm, relaxed and peaceful.

I joined a dance class, and even though I was a beginner, I found so much joy in learning a routine and applying myself in a way I'd not done for years. I felt alive. At times I couldn't keep up and remember the steps; I would often find myself going left when the rest of the dancers would go right – but it didn't matter because I was joyful with every step I took.

I felt alive. I even ended up doing things that I loved doing as a kid. I rode a bike again. I could feel myself again as a teenager, with the wind on my face, a wide smile, my feet off the pedals freewheeling. I even went rollerblading and played on the swings in the park. These things, however simple, gave me the opportunity to connect with the fun side, the light-hearted side of me, the one who wanted to have fun, who wanted to experience joy and with all this came a freer me. I was more open, and I was having fun just for fun. Although these were simple activities to do, the joy they brought was not; it was something far more fulfilling than that.

I gave myself permission to reconnect with my joyful self. The memories of innocence, playfulness and creativity brought me hope. I was nurturing myself, and in that came a greater sense of wellbeing and a lightness to my life. I started to move on from the things that had prevented me from participating in the joyful and passionate aspects of my soul. Even at work, I made decisions to stop doing work that didn't bring me joy. I did a full review of my life. I found myself with more time; those closest to me encouraged me even more to do things outside work and family that made me feel whole.

It was in these moments I realised I was healing. As part of my healing process, I decided to learn yoga and the principles that sat within a regular practice. I was keen to learn more about the Vedic traditions. I had tried yoga years ago, but it never quite sat with me. It wasn't high octane enough, but as I lay on the mat, listening to the twingy twangy music, I decided to keep an open mind. I was surrounded by young, nubile 20-somethings, all with svelte figures, stretching and warming up for the class ahead. I sat up and looked down at my midriff, immediately self-conscious. The mirrored wall to my right took no prisoners; my boobs were significantly lower and heavier than my fellow yogis, I looked like I'd been squashed into a square while everyone around me had been stretched; their elongated bodies never seemed to end. My critical companion chirped up; but I'd been practising mindfulness, so I chose to let the thought drift away immediately. To be honest, I was chuffed that I'd made it onto the mat. This was something I had also been practising – when a negative thought appeared, choosing to let it drift away and instead replace it with something positive. This, too, was bringing me joy.

The anticipation started to build in the studio; the music had changed to a folk song, the singer sang 'I like you, just the way you are.' Smiling, I lay back down on the mat; I had no idea what to expect. But the words of the song made me feel good, and I relaxed. The studio was packed; I was one of 40, and I was the eldest in the room. The yoga teacher entered the room, carefully stepping through the bodies to the front of the room, waving an incense stick to cleanse the air and to settle the room; the energy was electric. My desire for learning new things was once again confirmed.

We were asked to set our intention for the practice; silently, I said, 'to be present.' Next thing I was on my hands and knees doing cat, cow, then downward-facing dog, chaturanga, tree pose and a whole host of poses I didn't know, but I followed the instructions. I didn't realise I'd booked myself into the intermediate class, sweating and feeling very stretched, physically and emotionally; the instruction was for us all to move into savasana. What a relief to be back on my back. I lay there listening to the teacher guide us through a breathing process to ground us; I found myself drifting off. Three rounds of om at the end of the class before everyone was cleaning their mats, chatting quietly as they left the studio. I took my time, not sure if I'd liked my first proper yoga experience, pulled on my hoodie and headed home. I felt calm, at ease, and I smiled every step of the way home. This had also brought me joy. I booked myself in for two classes the very next week.

My newfound interest in yoga served me well. It allowed me to press the pause button in my weekly schedule; two hours a week, I found myself on the mat, learning the poses, being in the present, focusing on my breath and being grateful for these moments. I found my fellow yogis friendly; they'd say hello and ask how my week had been. The teachers and front desk assistants knew my name, and I felt welcomed. I belonged. I loved it, and I felt at peace.

When you give yourself permission to reconnect and establish what you want in your life, then it gives you the opportunity to connect with your joyful self. The world's wisdom traditions tell us that infinite delight and bliss reside within the very core of reality itself – within our core. Infinite joy is an inherent quality of our deepest being – we have just forgotten about it.

Delight and bliss now resided within the very core of me; it was inherent. Within my deepest being. I realised there was more I could do with my life, more I could do to help others, and I wrote another list and with that came a desire to learn even more new things.

That's when I trained to become a reiki healer, a Chopra Centre Meditation and Ayurveda teacher and I fell in love with yoga. I even started blogging and writing for fun. All this gave me even more energy, a zest for life beyond what I thought was possible. What struck me the most was how different I was; I was calmer, lighter and more grounded.

I had patience; I responded, not reacted; I laughed more. My work improved, and I attracted a whole host of new clients without really trying. I found my life started to flow more; it was easier, and over time abundance started to appear. Not just in money, but in the friendships and the relationships I had, and in the work I delivered. My sense of belonging in the community where I practised my yoga and my surroundings where I lived all became more vibrant, more interesting and more fulfilling.

From this came a healthier lifestyle, a healthier physical me and a healthier inner me. I was happy; I knew who I was and what I wanted in my life. I became more present. I stopped thinking too far ahead and instead found joy in everything I did. I went beyond the what if and found joy in what is.

I had forgotten that true joy comes from the very nature of who we are, and by reconnecting with that aspect of myself, joy started to unfold and manifest in my wider life. It felt that I was returning to wholeness; I was coming back home to my true self. Finding joy is an important step in your journey to coming home to your true self. We all have a deep longing for joy. When you invite it into your life, I would encourage you to honour that feeling. You now have the emotional freedom; use that space within wisely and let it give you the balance you need.

Exercise

To help you reconnect with your passions, consider the following questions:

- What makes you feel good?
- What makes you laugh?
- What excites you?
- What would you regret not trying?
- What would you do if you could do anything?

You could also try the following exercise.

Reconnect with a memory of something that brought you joy as a child. Imagine you are sitting in the cinema, and on the big screen is your memory playing out in front of you. What are you doing? Where were you? Who were you with? What are you seeing? What are you hearing? What are you feeling?

Reflect upon what you notice about your younger self, and what would that younger self say to you now?

Make a list of what you would like to reconnect with and do at least two things from your list and see how much joy it brings you.

8

CHAPTER 8

Experiential Living

'Be brave, take risks. Nothing can substitute experience.'

Paulo Coelho

Paulo Coelho said, 'Be brave, take risks. Nothing can substitute experience,' and as a person who learns through experience, this quote couldn't be truer for me.

When I introduced joy back into my life, I felt lighter; it was as if I had a newfound energy. Life did not feel as hard or such a struggle. It made me realise that by reconnecting with the things I felt passionate about, I somehow was introduced to new experiences, new people and a ton of new learning. I noticed I was stimulated, and the knowledge and experiences I was having were feeding my soul. Through this time of reconnection and coming home to my true self, it became apparent to me that nothing could substitute experiential living.

In 1943 Abraham Maslow was curious to learn what made emotionally fulfilled people tick. He studied many people, including Eleanor Roosevelt and Albert Einstein. He also looked at highly functioning college students poised to make their mark in the world. All those people he studied had the same thing in common; each person had robust self-esteem, felt a sense of belonging and were self-actualising their goals. He established that accomplishments and experiences – not things – made these people happy and fulfilled.

Since then, there have been many other studies by psychology professors, and Thomas Gilovich is one of them from Cornell University. He established through his research that experiences beat possessions, and that is because our memories of experiences tend to grow richer over time – even the negative ones. A disastrous trip, for example, could be framed over the years as a character-building experience. Despite the known benefits of experiential living, people still don't seem to fully embrace the ideal. Most of us have been there, buying material things, thinking it will provide us with a sense of satisfaction; this satisfaction is normally short-lived, and soon after, the purchase excitement starts to wear off.

Another way of putting this would be that in the short-term, our needs are met, but soon afterwards, we are looking for our next fix. Success of having a big new car, that big apartment, designer shoes, handbags and all the mod cons of modern-day living are all very good, but the question is… does it make you happy? Most would argue yes on the surface, but when probed further, will likely say 'not really.'

Happiness is mistakenly associated with owning possessions. But if longer-term happiness is to be found, it's necessary to go beyond modern-day human materialistic nature and make a conscious choice.

This is the difference between happiness and joy. Happiness is reactive; happiness comes and goes. It is an outward expression and can, at times, only last for a few minutes. Happiness relies on external achievements and materialistic gains, not on the experiences that create fulfilment. Although joy and happiness are different, it is good for us to still experience both, and without them, life would not be as much fun.

Happiness, we know, can mean very different things to different people and how to achieve it is a lifelong question for most of us. In Gilovich's study, he said, 'People often think spending money on an experience is not as wise an investment as spending it on material possessions. They think the experience will come and go in a flash, and they'll be left with little compared to owning an item. But we remember experiences long afterward, as we become used to our possessions. At the same time, we also enjoy the anticipation of having an experience more than the anticipation of owning a possession.'

The experiences we have reflect who we really are; they take us closer to our true selves. When these experiences are shared, they allow us to connect to our authenticity, to others, and the world around us. The experiences will become meaningful and significant.

My dad once said, 'Money can't buy you happiness,' and he was right. In one way, it doesn't, but without money, we wouldn't be happy either. We have to have money to live and function in the world we live in. But when money is the sole focus, or material things and possessions become the most important things in our lives, we lose the ability to have balance. We cannot see beyond the next quick fix.

Those who chase money believe that valuable people are those that earn more money, have more fame and get more respect. But chasing any of these things will not make you happy. It won't make you feel satisfied, as you will need to keep feeding the belief. In the long-term, the pursuit of materialistic things can make you less satisfied and less fulfilled. In the longer-term, it can make you poorer when it comes to the deeper currency that is required to enjoy a contented life.

It is difficult because focusing on what you want, rather than what you currently have, can make it impossible to appreciate what's already in your life. Finding an inner balance is essential. If we don't, we will never live our life's purpose, and we won't find our way home. We will always be searching for something that is unobtainable or will inevitably end up as a quick fix. We must experience a life that goes beyond materialistic living and instead tune in to the experience's life has to offer.

Tuning in will guide you and eventually shape how you live your life. Experiential living will introduce you to different worldly perspectives. They will transform your life and teach you how to be humble, virtuous and compassionate. More importantly, experiential living will give you many gifts that you won't acquire anywhere else.

This is all very easy to say but doing it and sticking to it is not always as easy. In my late twenties, when married to my first husband, I found myself living a life that could only be described as keeping up with the Joneses. From the outside looking in, it appeared we had everything. Flashy cars. A lovely, big home and nice clothes. I was caught up in a way of living that I thought made me happy. Fancy dinners, expensive holidays and showing off what we had. Every couple of years, we would upgrade our lifestyle, which included new jobs, new possessions and new homes.

Nothing could get in the way of us spending and living a life that was so focused on what we had. We didn't even realise how unhappy we were. Without those things, quick fixes, we couldn't see that we were living a lie. A big pretence, showing externally to the world we had everything we needed, a fake existence that permeated everything we did. This was not my way; I had not been brought up to be so focused on material things, but there I was sucked in playing one of my many roles.

Through this bred a level of contempt. Over time came a shimmer of disrespect, and overall, none of our personal needs were being met. Throughout this period, my husband changed, and so did I. We started to drift apart and what motivated us and drove us became very different. Money was not my be all and end all. I didn't want to keep living in the way we did. Don't get me wrong, there is nothing wrong in working hard and having money, but if the money you are spending is masking a deeper fundamental issue, then that will not offer you a healthy and happy life. My relationship with my ex-husband had been fractured for many years prior to my wake-up call, and when I realised we wanted different things, it was difficult to keep pretending everything was rosy. As my realisation came, so did the recession in early 2008. This put the world in a spin, equally as it did us.

Four years earlier, I had started my first business. It was at this point things started to change for me. I made a conscious decision that I needed to change. I was unhappy in my job, and so I embarked on a life coaching programme mainly to help me figure out what I needed to do in my own life to make the changes I wanted to make. With that came a whole new understanding of what was important to me, how I could live my life, and I started to build a new relationship with myself. It felt good. I felt good, and soon after that came my vision for wanting to help others do the same. In 2004, I set up a small coaching practice where I would help others in the way I had been helped. My focus turned to helping others, and with that came a sense of happiness, fulfilment and I was grateful for being able to do this kind of work and get paid for it. With any business, it has its ups and downs, and cash flow was tight. But over the years, the creases of a growing business were ironed out, and I was being rewarded in many ways. I had a richness in the work I did, the team I employed and a richness in a more honest life that I was living.

What I hadn't addressed was my relationship with my husband, and his needs and drivers. Over the first four years of running my business they had an impact on our bottom line. I didn't want to walk away from my relationship. I had made a vow to work and commit to our life. We had our son, and life with the business was challenging enough. Over the three years that led to my wake-up call, my relationship descended to one of despair, deep frustration, and unhappiness. The turmoil generated was unhealthy and bittersweet. I had my dream job, but my relationship was at an all-time low. I tried to change our lifestyle so we didn't need to keep up with the Joneses any longer. My husband had joined the business and was now active in trying to run it, and this made our work and home situation even worse. The dynamic I was caught up in led me straight to my wake-up call three years later.

When the recession hit, life needed to be significantly different. But in all honesty, I didn't realise the enormity of it at the time. The business was extremely successful, perhaps one of the most regarded coach training companies in the UK at the time. But as the recession continued into late 2009, clients stopped paying, corporate work dried up, and unrest was everywhere. No one felt secure. Life got very challenging; the business was spending more than it was earning, and with the staff, wages and office to keep, things had to change dramatically. I didn't want to keep pretending everything was rosy when behind the scenes we were living on our overdraft. We were living beyond our means personally and professionally. Trying to survive a global crisis and keep everything afloat meant more loans and a bigger overdraft in the hope we would survive.

During all the chaos, we decided to separate. This was a joint decision to see how living apart would work. What seemed like an amicable decision soon turned out to be like the War of the Roses. Later that year and early into the next, when the lawyers had done their damage, and my ex-husband had recouped as much money as he could, I was left with no other option but to liquidise any assets that I had left.

What led to the tsunami was years of living a lie. Focusing on monetary gain was my ex-husband's path, but I had chosen to walk that path, too, even though I knew it was not where I belonged. Ten years of marriage and everything I had worked to create became a commercial transaction. All was gone.

The runaway train I'd been on for the last seven years screeched to a halt. I flew head-on into unknown territory with a noose of a debt that did not fully belong to me around my neck. With my marriage, home and my business gone, I was spat out with no materialistic things to hold on to. All of what I had was gone. Within a few months, the friends I thought were friends, including the small team that I had to let go, distanced themselves from me. Some even crossed the road when they saw me coming. I could no longer keep up with the lifestyle they had or the expectation they required from me. The shame of what happened made people distant.

When the tsunami had died down, in all my turmoil, the angst, worry and not knowing what to do or where to start came my greatest strength, and that has led me to where I am now – a decade later.

I found a rented apartment with the kindest Italian lady living in the apartment below. I'd come home from work with delicious, home-cooked food on the doorstep and bowls of popcorn for my son. I reached out to all my students and clients and explained what had happened and honoured the work they had paid for; it took me six months to deliver on this, but I did it, and it felt good. I started to rebuild my life and pay the debt off month by month. I would do what was right, and I would clear the debt, and in that process, clear my name.

I cherished the moments I had with my son and created a home, one that was stable, honest and loving. I went back to basics, started a new coaching and coach training practice and over the years built it back up to be what it was meant to be. It was in this phase of rebuilding when I started my quest to find myself again, to experience life in a way that had meaning to me but also to others.

I found love, a true love, one with shared values, shared beliefs, one of kindness and of a deep connection.

I simplified my life; I decluttered everything. I learned to live every experience as they came, some were good, and some were not so good. But with every experience, I learned from them. Years later, when I reconnected with the lighter side of myself, I took time to reflect on my experiences. Money didn't buy me happiness. But losing it and then the experience of rebuilding and creating a life I was meant to lead did. For that, I am eternally grateful. It has been one of the greatest gifts I've been given so far.

The experiences we have in life, those you may have in yours, are important, pinnacle experiences. No matter how small or large, they will make an impact on who you become. We all are thrown curveballs. We are all driven and motivated by different things. We all have experiences, good and bad, but if we can find inspiration in overcoming adverse situations, then we will find the key to genuine contentment in life.

Experiences are unforgettable; they are joyful, exciting and at times challenging. They teach you important lessons that will give you purpose and lead you to find your passion. You will then be offered the opportunity to live in your greatest potential.

Why am I telling you this story? Because in all my loss, I found abundance by experientially living. I, like we all need to, earned money and eventually that money allowed me to buy a home for my son. Even though money still makes the world go round, my relationship with it changed. I no longer needed the possessions I once wanted. My focus shifted, and instead, I had a richness way beyond money.

I found that through the work I did, the relationships I'd cultivated with myself and others, and my new way of approaching my life meant that I got more and more. I was thankful for these moments and showed gratitude.

Cultivating rich experiences can create memories that last long after the novelty of a new possession wears off. Spending your time experientially living, that uses fewer resources and has spiritual and physical benefits will allow you to live a more fulfilled and abundant life. The experiences you have will not be quick fixes to fill the void of what's missing in your life. Instead, they will enrich your life and give you the gift of true abundance.

True abundance shows up in the simple things such as being outside in nature, going for a hike or a cycle. It can be playing games with your children or even cuddling up to your loved one on the sofa. It could also be travelling to amazing parts of the world, going to a sporting event, or a friend's wedding.

Abundance comes from within, not with the purchase of possessions. Those that live a life beyond the surface will find abundance in the experiences of their life. You don't have to lose everything to find abundance. But a review of what's important in your life is necessary. Where do you place value? The experience or the possession?

Living an abundant life can start now, you do not need to wait until it knocks you off your feet. You can start cultivating it now, followed by embodying it.

Exercise

Consider the following questions:

- When feeling dissatisfied with life – what's your go-to?

- What drives you to buy new possessions?

- What materialistic things do you rely on to make you happy?

- How much of your life is focused on experiential living, and why?

- Does your life feel balanced – getting the right number of experiences?

- What could you let go of to create more space for experiential living?

8

CHAPTER 9

Using Your Gifts And Talents Creatively

'Success now and in the future comes from being more yourself. If you are willing to express your uniqueness, you will contribute something of real value to the world.'

Richard Koch

The next step in our journey is mastering our creativity, natural gifts and talents. Over 50% of the population don't know what their gifts or talents are, never mind use them. Coming home to your true self requires you to acknowledge all the things that are unique to you, your talents, strengths, and gifts. We tend to go through life doing, and not always recognising what comes easy or even is effortless. By using your natural gifts and talents, you bring creativity into your life. At the start of this book, I talked about you already being perfection; this is the same thing. We forget what is within us, what is within our gift.

We are born with an innate set of gifts and talents, and when you use them in your everyday life, you can design the life you want to live. Remember, we are resourceful and creative. Everything we need already resides within.

We are nearly home, back home to your true self. Meaning this phase of the journey, like all, is an important one. Without being able to tap into your unique gifts and talents, you won't be able to live your life using them.

So how do you tap into your gifts, talents and your creativity?

Firstly, you need to know what you're good at. By focusing on the experiences you have in your everyday life, you should be starting to build a picture of how you are in those experiences; who do you see? What do you do? How do you experience your experiences? All these aspects of who you are and what you do can go unnoticed. But when you start to witness what you do and observe, you gradually start to notice yourself, and in those moments, you can determine what comes naturally to you.

Would you describe yourself as a person who can communicate well? One who sends a clear message and those you speak to understand you?

Are you a person who is awesome at problem-solving; you get to the heart of an issue, analyse the data, figure out how to tackle it and then find a solution?

Or are you a person who cares for others, shows empathy and compassion in a way that goes beyond the norm?

We all have a set of innate talents and gifts that are unique to us. We were born with them. Some of these gifts and talents are developed already, and others are waiting to be discovered. You have already learned so much about yourself, who you are, what you want, and now as we move into the final phases of this journey together, you need to understand how your gifts and talents can be used creatively. Not only to help you create the life you want to live but to help and support those around you. Allowing others to be touched by your gifts and talents will bring more abundance, joy and fulfilment into your life.

When we immediately think about creativity, most assume creative people are artists, actors, musicians, or writers, and yes, these are creative people that produce a creative output. Yet, this should not stop us from tuning into our personal creativity.

Creativity does not have to always be in such a defined way. Creativity is not an elite or even prestigious way of being. It does not have to be so far removed from everyday living. For example, you could take an idea from the history of ancient Greece and apply the philosophy to the running of a business or school. Essentially, creativity means spotting an opportunity to improve things through recombination. And that recombination means using your gifts and talents. When we do this, we can make a real difference to the world if we use them creatively.

Using our gifts and talents creatively is not just for our sole enjoyment; they are meant to be shared with others. Research shows that when we use our talents and gifts in our everyday lives, doing what we do best brings inner happiness and contentment.

Going back to only 50% of humans knowing what their talents are, never mind living them, shows that most of the population haven't yet realised what their gifts and talents are.

When we start to explore this side of ourselves, it is easy to fall into the trap of limited thinking. I've been asked many times, 'Yeah, that would be great to use my talents every day, but how does that pay the rent?' A fine question to ask, but you are not expected to give up your job and not have a salary. We're talking about fully using your gifts and talents in everything you do.

This should not be about having something extra to do; this is simply about fully showing up in your own life and sharing your uniqueness.

Richard Koch said from the 80/20 principle, 'Success now and in the future comes from being more yourself. If you are willing to express your uniqueness, you will contribute something of real value to the world.'

This quote has stayed with me over the last decade, and for me, this is essential to coming home to your true self. You need to know what you can offer the world.

In my case, I realised I loved designing training courses. I was excellent at listening and I was intuitive. When I used that talent, I helped my clients make significant changes in their lives. When I sat down to write a new life or professional development programme, I created a magical, experiential programme that would help others change their lives for the good. But when I delivered it, there was even more magic – it was transformational in every way. Over time, with more study, I realised I could help others heal, and through the process of supporting others, I used this gift wisely, but also generously. This then became my business. I combined everything I knew I was good at and crafted a business around it.

I'm good at photography, and this is something I've fallen back into. I do this for the sheer pleasure of doing it. I share my work with my family and friends, and they love what I produce for them. The photos bring them joy and often puts smiles on their faces. Which, in return, does the same for me too.

Our gifts and talents are purposely created not just for ourselves but to help those around us. We benefit from other people's talents all the time, but many of us don't take the time to notice these benefits – we tend to take things for granted. Yet, we've all benefited from Edison's light bulb. Ford's automotive ideas and even Alexander Graham Bell's telephone – what would we do without that gift? Almost everyone around us contributes to the welfare of others one way or another.

So, how do other people benefit from your gifts and talents? Imagine a world if no one shared their talents. It would be pretty bland. Think about it for a moment, when you cook a meal for your family or friends – are you cooking it for your sole enjoyment, or do you get delight in watching everyone else enjoy the meal you have prepared and created?

There is no sense of delight when we only serve ourselves. So, sharing our talents with other people can create more lasting fulfilment. Sharing your talents and gifts when other people receive a benefit from it – well, it's a win-win situation all round.

The key to successfully doing this is quite simple, but one many forget. There is one unspoken rule, and that is, do not seek or wait for recognition. You are sharing your gifts not to be recognised;

you are not attached to the outcome, meaning you should not be seeking approval, acceptance, or praise from other people.

You are sharing your gifts and talents because you know it can help, support, or bring joy to others. If we seek recognition, or we are focused on getting something back from sharing our talents, then we know our ego is back in play. The greatest gift you can give yourself is to share yourself with others and not expect anything back in return. By doing this, we can have an even more satisfying life.

There has been some amazing research done by Gallup, who also believe that if you use your strengths, talents and gifts – something that comes naturally that can be enhanced through practise every day – your health and wellness will improve.

Those they researched said they experienced less worry, stress, anger, sadness and physical pain. We know already from the work we have been doing that if you are not aligned and feeling good from within, your physicality will start to suffer.

Using what is unique to you and what comes naturally to you will bring higher levels of positive emotions and more energy. You will wake up feeling energised and excited about the day ahead, and your overall engagement levels will be significantly higher. Your cornerstones of wellness will flourish. You will have a joyful energetic body, a compassionate, loving heart, a reflective, alert mind, and finally will find lightness in your being.

This is within your reach if you want it. Living in this way can give you a richness, an abundance in life beyond what you could imagine. We don't want to take any credit for our talents, but it's how we use them that counts. There are always opportunities waiting for each of us; we just need to be receptive and open to seeing them. Most of us don't always see those opportunities, even if they are in front of our noses.

As humans, we overthink, over analyse and push things to happen. When we do this, we are not in our most grounded state. Which means we are not open to opportunity presenting itself. This takes us back to our golden thread and being aligned. Ensuring your mind, heart and will are all open and remain open. Being open to share a thought, an idea without an agenda. To share your talents or gifts will, for sure, touch others in some way, shape or form. There is something about giving unconditionally that is yours to give, which will create something of real beauty. A union of body, mind and spirit, between giver and receiver. Knowing that the gift you give will be received graciously and willingly.

You have been given these gifts and talents in the first instance, they are innate, and they are unique to you and only you. Although others may have similar gifts and talents to you, it is how you use them that makes them unique to you.

You need to unearth them; dig deep to discover what they are. No one can do this for you; only you know where they're hidden. Once you do find them, you need to let them shine, using them whenever you can.

The more you use your unique talents and gifts, the more opportunity you will have to let them shine even brighter. You will be blessed with opportunities to use them, and you will find yourself fulfilled. Living your dharma – your purpose.

I encourage you to tune in to what naturally comes easy to you. Try and use your innate gifts and talents in every opportunity you can.

Exercise

Make a list of your talents, strengths and innate gifts.

- How often do you use them?

- When you do use them, how do you feel – what happens to you?

- How can you use these more in your life?

- What can you create by using your talents, strengths and innate gifts?

- How would you like to express your talents, strengths and innate gifts?

- How could you share your talents, strengths and innate gifts?

- How can you use these with your family and friends?

- How can you use these in the work you do?

- How can you use these in your community?

- Can you use your uniqueness to create something of real value in the world?

CHAPTER 10

Self-Care

'Nothing can bring you peace but yourself.'

Ralph Waldo Emerson

We're coming towards the end of our journey, and our destination is on the horizon. As we move into the final stages of our journey, we need to master self-care. I call this 'topping up your tank.'

It's important to recognise when your energy levels are depleting and what works for you in relation to your own self-care. We started our journey with learning to quieten the mind, and we know that meditation is one of the techniques we can use in our self-care routine. In the Vedic tradition, Dinacharya is the term for a daily lifestyle routine. When creating a self-care strategy, it's important that it can be sustained. You have already done so much work on yourself. If we want to sustain the progress you've made so far, it's essential you start to implement a daily lifestyle routine. Something that is manageable and also something that will allow you to feel rested and rejuvenated.

The process of walking yourself back home requires you to commit to a lifelong journey of self-discovery. It requires regular check-ins as to where you are, what's happening within you and around you. Along with deepening your relationship with yourself, it will keep you on the path to wholeness. When you create a daily lifestyle routine, things you integrate into your life will have a huge impact on how you feel about your world.

Self-care is one of those topics that can be labelled as being selfish, but in fact, it's completely the opposite of that. Self-care is the key to a long, healthy and vibrant life. Now that you have space in your backpack, you can start to think about your self-care routine and what's going to work for you. We have one body that we occupy from the moment of our birth to the moment of our death. It's important not to misuse it or take it for granted. Honouring your mind, body and soul are the keys to taking care of the whole of you and mastering this lesson: recognising when your energy levels are depleted; understanding what you need at certain times of your day to support a balanced and energised body; and knowing when you need to give yourself compassion to support your mind or calm your emotions.

This requires you to take care of the whole of you, and by doing this, you can start to understand the four cornerstones of wellness.

These cornerstones are known as the physical, the emotional, the mental and the spiritual. When introducing these four cornerstones into your life, you start to cultivate a new way of living.

When you finally come home to your true self, you will have learned how to honour your whole self. Life beyond this can be lived effortlessly, with ease and grace. This is where a daily lifestyle routine comes in. Without this, it will be easy for you to go back into old habits, old ways of living and thinking. We do not want you to disconnect from your golden thread.

In the last chapter, we explored using your gifts and talents and sharing those with others. One of the challenges of doing this could lead to you giving too much of yourself to others. This is one of the biggest issues we have when it comes to our self-care – we prioritise others before ourselves. Usually, we tend to be on the bottom of the list, and our self-care gets forgotten about.

I have spent most of my life being one of those people. Doing too much for others and not enough for myself. When you are forced to stop and take stock of your life, you quickly realise that you weren't even on the list to begin with, never mind being at the bottom of it.

One of the laws of the universe focuses on the exchange of giving and receiving. It's important that you find ways that can create an equal balance. The universe operates through this dynamic exchange of giving and receiving, and the same applies to our wellbeing.

If you get a deep sense of satisfaction in giving to others, you may find that you could be giving too much and not receiving enough in return. Unable to top up your own tank. It can also work the opposite way. You may find yourself taking too much from others and not giving enough back in return. Either way, if there is no equilibrium, you will be out of balance.

To live your life in flow, with ease and grace, you need to master balancing between giving and receiving. When you do one more than the other, you will find it difficult to ground yourself and remain centred. This can show up in many ways. You may recognise that something just doesn't feel right. You will be out of sorts; you will feel under the weather, and fatigue will kick in. It's in these moments you need to understand how much you are giving versus how much you are receiving. It is essential you learn to understand what you need and when you need it. Without that inner strength or resilience, it's unlikely you will ever come fully home because you'll be too exhausted to get there.

Most of us think we should look after ourselves, do an exercise class, or go for a run, go on a diet, cut out the carbs, stop drinking. But when we put restrictions on ourselves, and we only deal with what we think we should do, we're only dealing with the symptom. We are not getting to the root cause.

I, like many, approached my self-care with the 'I should' attitude rather than the 'I know' attitude, which led me to be on a diet for over 20 years of my life. Most women I know are always criticising how big their bum looks or how bloated their belly is. No one says I love my body. Watching my mum yo-yo diet influenced how I felt about my body too. We forget that we have had role models, and if you're a parent too, you too will be a role model. All of us are influenced by good and bad body images. I had never been confident about my body, but after my sexual assault, I felt less confident and was ashamed of how my body looked. Being naked is something I've shied away from, even with my most intimate life partners. I always admired those women in the gym changing rooms who could walk around freely, showing off all they had without a flicker of embarrassment. I would be wrapped in my towel, struggling to put my pants and bra on with one hand. I'd have a sweat on, defeating the object of having a shower.

The interesting thing about this is that I have never been big, but I have never been skinny. I am your average woman; curvy is how my body type would be described. When I was pregnant with my son, I ate for two, literally. My restrictive eating regime was lifted, and I gave myself permission to eat what I wanted. Cake, cookies, sweet treats, savoury treats, you name it, I shovelled it in. I had an excuse; I was, after all, eating for two.

Although through my pregnancy I was OK with this, once my son was born, I became even more self-conscious and, dare I say, appalled at my body. This time my boobs were heavier, fuller than before, and I had become square in appearance; there was no going in at the waist. I was a cube of excess soft, flabby skin. My face had always been round, but now it was like the moon. For the first year, I couldn't shift the weight, but over time, the pounds gradually started to drop off.

When the cracks in my first marriage started to appear, I noticed that the self-care routine I had been following started to fall by the wayside. I found I didn't have the energy to go to the gym; I noticed I would opt for sweet treats instead of a healthy alternative. My good work and commitment were waning. My alcohol intake increased, which made me want to eat easy, comfort food and the daily routine I had put into place was soon forgotten. I was irritable, lacking in energy and felt completely out of balance. I knew something was wrong but didn't have the energy to fight it. This went on for a number of years, and so did my habits.

I needed to lose three stone. The thought overwhelmed me, and I was not enthused about the task ahead. I was going to the gym three times a week, eating my five a day and drinking my required water – but nothing was shifting. I taught others how to create a transformational goal, and I figured I needed to create one for myself. I needed to set myself a goal that would motivate and energise me. The first goal I set myself was: *I'm wearing Prada with pride.* This is maybe a silly goal to some, but to me, it was meaningful. It meant I would feel good in my skin. I would be confident within myself and would be proud of my body. I took the principles of coaching and applied them to my situation.

Small baby steps to begin with, and with that came a clear idea of what I needed to do. I didn't need to just lose the weight, I needed to focus on my self-care. I looked beyond the weight, and I decided to explore all four cornerstones. I had been introduced to the concept of the six pillars of health from Deepak Chopra on my Ayurveda teacher training, and I knew I had to apply and integrate these into my life. Sleep, meditation, mindful movement, healthy emotions, grounding and optimal nutrition.

One of the ways of maintaining your self-care is the introduction of a daily routine. Creating a healthy daily routine by aligning ourselves with nature's rhythms and honouring its cycles of rest and activity are critical to finding balance. In today's world, many of us are unaware of the natural rhythms of our body and are guided instead by habit and convenience. We ignore the internal signals and rely on the external ones. The result is often compromised health. Fatigue and the accumulation of toxicity builds in our body and mind. All leading to a range of symptoms most experience daily. Anxiety, insomnia, physical ailments such as migraines, muscle pain, dizziness. Racing thoughts, constant worrying, difficulty concentrating and making decisions. These are real, modern-day challenges that stop self-care. When exploring the four cornerstones of wellness, I set about tackling them one by one.

I chose to look after the whole of me, the physical, the emotional, the mental and the spiritual aspects of myself. I decided to craft my own self-care strategy. I needed to look at my routine. I decided to explore what my routine should look like and what was realistic and manageable for me. My self-care strategy was to have:

1. A joyful, energetic body

2. A compassionate, loving heart

3. A reflective, alert mind

4. A lightness of being

To create a joyful, energetic body, I continued with my physical activity. Along with my yoga and going to the gym, I also opted for walking in nature, cycling and running. There was something about being outside in nature that made my mood lighter, and I found myself more energised. I noticed that I stopped craving the sweet things, and instead, my palate craved healthier alternatives. More fruit, more vegetables and lean proteins. I stopped drinking alcohol, and I immediately had more energy, and my hormonal mood swings stopped. I developed an evening routine where my phone would be out of reach after 8pm. No scrolling was allowed. I would light a candle in the bedroom, spray the pillows with aromatics, and the lights would be out by 10.30pm. I made sure I got eight hours of undisturbed sleep every night, even at the weekends.

Within a month of introducing this routine into my life, the weight started to move. A few pounds to begin with, but each week and month that passed by, more weight shifted. I was learning to manage my energy better in terms of what I was giving versus receiving, and I found myself regaining balance. When I looked at my body, I felt no shame or embarrassment. I started to build a better relationship with the physical aspects of my being. My body was joyful and energetic, and I loved it.

Exercise

Cultivate your daily routine. Write down your ideal and put it into practice. Include exercise, mealtimes, wake-up and lights out times. Stop using your phone as a distraction and create a welcoming night-time ritual. Compliment your body and be wary of the balance between giving and receiving. Each day get outside in nature for at least 15 minutes. Manage your food intake and try new foods; eat at the same time every day. Your latest meal should be no later than 7pm and your biggest meal of the day should be eaten at lunchtime between 12–1 pm.

This will help you develop a joyful, energetic body.

To create a compassionate, loving heart, I continued to build upon the work I had done already on my compassionate observer of self. I had been practising meditation, and this was going well, but I also introduced reiki into my monthly routine. This helped me with my balance, and I noticed how I experienced my world was different. I observed without judgment. I acknowledged if I was having a bad day, and I learned to change my relationship with life challenges. When those challenges presented themselves, I would repeat quietly, 'I love all resistance to all illusion.' In these moments, I could respond instead of reacting.

I saw only the good in the challenge or the resistance. I would compassionately welcome it and know in all of it, there was something for me to learn, and I would grow from the experiences. My patience and tolerance expanded, and I accepted myself fully. Each day after my meditation practice, I would breathe consciously for a few extra minutes. I would repeat the mantra, 'I am whole; I am creative, and I am resourceful. I love you, Gillian.' I had developed a compassionate, loving heart.

Exercise

Before reacting, try to tune in to your body's inner wisdom – we all have it. As you consider the choice before you, pay attention to the sensations in your body and use the feelings of comfort or discomfort to guide you. Most people receive the message of comfort or discomfort around the heart. Others receive the message in their solar plexus and others in their 'gut feeling' in their belly. Putting your attention on your heart or gut, ask your body, 'How do I feel about this choice?'

If your body sends a feeling of comfort and eagerness, you can plunge ahead. If your body sends a signal of physical or emotional distress, then it isn't the optimal choice. Pause and consider other possibilities until you find a choice that resonates with your heart's guidance. Try it and see if this helps in those moments.

The aim is to connect more with yourself when emotions rise, so you can self-regulate, as when you do, you will be able to proceed with awareness and compassion. You will have a centred awareness that can aid you when your emotions arise. This will help you develop a compassionate, loving heart.

To create a reflective alert mind, I remained positive. My mindset was open, and I learned how to become more mindful in everything I did. One of the ways I did this was decluttering. I learned how to decompress throughout my day, not just when I left work. I introduced conscious breathing and pauses for breath four times a day. I would also bring my attention into my body and become aware of the movements, energy and feelings that I experienced. I would get up and walk every hour and stretch. Being aware of my body, breath and introducing regular pauses were immediately freeing. I had more clarity and more focus.

My capacity for learning increased, and my decision making was precise. My creativity and problem solving shifted into a new gear, and I had carved out time for reflection. Integrating mini-breaks throughout my day helped refresh my mind and body. Over time I developed a reflective, alert mind.

Exercise

Consider the following questions:

- What you do to rest your mind during and after a workday?
- What helps you tune out the noise?

Throughout your day, try stretching or taking a brief walk, even if it's only a few feet away. Get yourself a drink of water, talk to a friend, get in touch with a loved one, even if it's just a text. If you can't do that purposely, look at photos that have special meaning. The brain needs those pauses.

Try unplugging for an hour every couple of days. Switch every device you have onto aeroplane mode and free yourself from the constant bings of social media and email.

We also need to know how to debrief from a day's work. That might mean walking home from work to clear your head, driving in silence or listening to music to help transition from work to home. There are several other ways that may help calm mental activity. If you find yourself working from home, make sure you have a clear distinction between home and work. Play your favourite song loud as you close your computer. Clear your desk and order your papers for the next day. This ritual is essential to help you transition from work to home. Be clear about finishing time – when you stop – you stop.

Another way to separate work from home is to have a shower. In the ancient Vedic tradition, a shower will wash away the day and any negative energy and toxic thoughts. As the water cleanses your mind, body and emotions, you can enter your evening free from the day.

To have a reflective, alert mind, you need mental freedom, so try and create some new routines that can help you do this.

To create a lightness of being felt less tangible as I was moving into a state of being. I continued with my meditation but increased it to twice a day for 30 mins. I started to introduce a conscious approach to gratitude. When things happened throughout my day, I would be thankful. Each night I would keep a gratitude journal; I would acknowledge, be thankful and write what I appreciated about my day, others and myself. I would actively seek out those I wanted to say thank you to. I would be clear about the message I wanted to share and actively say, 'I acknowledge you, and I am thankful for you.' The peace that came with these simple acts of kindness was something I hadn't experienced before. What I noticed was that others would start making similar comments back to me. The universal currency was in flow – the giving and receiving were reciprocal. I hadn't expected it or even wanted it, but when it came, I showed gratitude.

I decided to test out smiling to those I passed on the street. At first, it was a bit strange, but again the more I did this, the more people smiled back. The connection momentarily was made; even after I had walked by the smile remained on my face, and I am sure it did on those I passed. I ventured into saying good morning or good afternoon, and this, too, was well received.

On my daily walks, I slowed down. I noticed the sky, the clouds, the wind blowing through the trees, and I started to pay attention to the subtle shifts in temperature. When the sun shined, I tilted my face upwards to the sky to feel the warmth, and it felt like I had been kissed by mother nature. I felt connected to something bigger than me.

I introduced daily intentions into my morning routine on how I wanted to be, how I wanted to show up. This made me even more connected – my intention to simply be present. I focused on the moment, not the past or the future, just what was happening right here, right now.

Exercise

I invite you to set your intention daily, slow down when you are doing your activities and notice the subtle shifts that appear around you. Openly connect with others and acknowledge them and show gratitude where possible. Commit to a gratitude journal – write what you have appreciated about your day, others and yourself.

If you master these four cornerstones, you will be able to top up your tank as and when you need to. You will become the master of your own self-care. For this to become integrated – part of who you are – you will need to practise these regularly.

Self-care is not selfish; it is essential to living and honouring who you are. Make time for all four cornerstones and experience first-hand how your return to wholeness emerges.

8

CHAPTER 11

Finding Your Purpose

'The two most important days in your life are the day you are born and the day you find out why.'

Mark Twain

As we move into the penultimate lesson of this journey, it's important that we turn our focus to articulating exactly what our purpose is. So that when we arrive home, we have everything we need for us to live the life that we are meant to live.

You have decided what you want to take with you in your backpack. You have developed and started to implement your self-care strategy. Now you need to determine your purpose.

You have done so much work to get here and have already achieved so much. It is at this stage of the journey where you need to ground all your learning and put the spotlight on your purpose.

Purpose defines who you are; it reflects your passions and values. It provides clarity as you set goals and take action. Your sense of purpose steers how you live your life and how you lead yourself and others. If we really want something, we can have it – we can achieve whatever we want to. By now, you will have realised that if you put your mind to something, you can achieve it. Like everything you have done so far, all you need to do is keep your focus and belief in yourself. Trust that you can do it.

The most authentic brands are always built from the inside out. They're authentic and real. When you embrace personal purpose to identify and capture who you really are, what you stand for, and live this every day, you will inspire, motivate and make an impact in your life.

Another way of looking at finding your purpose is finding your calling. Call it faith, mindfulness, or whatever it is you wish to align yourself with. This anchoring makes it possible to navigate through life. You are able to visualise your existence for a specific reason.

Finding your purpose in life feels huge and difficult, but it's not as hard as you think. All you have to do is know where to look. Some know from a very early age what they are destined for – a surgeon, a scientist, a musician – but most people have to search for it, longing to articulate it, asking themselves, 'Who am I, and what am I here for?' Finding the answer to those questions will lead you home, back to your true self.

We are all born with a purpose, and we are all on a journey to follow our path. Purpose in life is known as dharma, and the law of dharma states that everyone has a purpose in life. We all have our own unique gifts and talents, and if we use these unique attributes in all aspects of our life and these are expressed and then shared with those who need it or with those who will benefit from it, then your dharma, your purpose, can be realised. That's why we have been discovering what our gifts and talents are.

We were all created to live our purpose; we are all here for a reason, and we all have a path to walk. Sages, gurus, spiritual teachers share the same philosophy. Knowing we are all created to live our purpose. While living your purpose doesn't always guarantee a lavish lifestyle, it will offer you to be part of something bigger than yourself. You will be part of something that positively impacts the world and leaves a legacy behind for the future generation.

Living your life's purpose does not mean we have to conquer the world, find a cure for cancer or live our life like a saint. But what it does mean is that we should embrace what feels right to us. And that's why we need to master this next step in our journey.

Once you have declared what your purpose is and you start to walk your path, you will find all the worry, the frustration and the conflict you have had in your life will start to drift away. It will allow you to step fully into your potential, you will be self-actualising, and you will become what you were born to be.

We all have the potential and the opportunity to do something with it, but research shows that only 10% of our human potential is ever fully realised, and the 90% that's left tends to lie dormant within us. There are many reasons that stop us from reaching our potential, but the biggest reason is ourselves. As we have discovered, we are the roadblock that stops us and makes it difficult for ourselves.

It is, however, within our gift. To move into a place within our lives where we can reach self-actualisation, we just need to have the courage and belief. There is no set manual or rules carved in stone to tell you how you should live your life on purpose and live life within your potential because your journey is unique to you. It is your path, your purpose and your potential.

When living a life with purpose, you are aligned. The mind is open, your heart is open, and you are willing. There is an intrinsic connection between your purpose, passion and wellbeing. When embracing your life in this way, you will be joyful and have hope. You will be optimistic and find a deep sense of fulfilment, contentment and gratitude.

Once we open ourselves up to this optimal life experience, we open the door of possibility in our own lives. You can achieve your dreams and make a positive impact on those around you. Remember, to live a life on purpose and self-actualise it does not mean you have to be a rocket scientist; all you need to do is be you.

Your purpose is who you are and what makes you, YOU. Purpose defines who you are; it reflects your strengths, passions and values. It will provide you with the clarity you need to set your inner compass to navigate you to your true path. Your sense of purpose steers how you want your story to go and how you lead your life.

You could find joy in achieving mastery in a niche hobby. You could be a parent who gets purpose from raising their children to be a positive force in the world. Or an employee who uses their ever-increasing skills to improve the lives of others.

When you wake up and realise there is something more for you in life, something more you can offer the world, something more purposeful, that is good for you but also will be good for others, you start to pay attention, in a way you've never been able to do before. The fog lifts, and for the first time in your life, you can see clearly. Everything is more vibrant and has more meaning. This is when the universe offers a helping hand – synchronicity and all that we want falls into place. You will be guided gently to your true path, and opportunities will present themselves for you to live your purpose.

Living your dharma is the single most important thing you can do in your life. It's not *what* you do; it's *how* you do it and *why* – the strengths and passions that define you. It will feel like coming home.

As you move into this phase of your journey, you may be challenged by others. You may receive powerful messages from partners, parents, bosses, friends, or the media about what you should be doing and how you should be doing it. Remember, this is not being selfish; this is living life being true to you. It is about coming home to your true self, peeling back the layers and embracing the whole of you and then living it – every single day. The only person you can be is yourself, be nobody but yourself. Choose to live life in your dharma and walk the path you are meant to walk. Have faith in yourself, and even if, at times, it's challenging, it feels a little overwhelming or you are having a crisis of confidence – you've got this. You can do this. If I can, so can you.

When I embraced my purpose, my world changed instantly. The awakening to my purpose in life was not that far off what I was doing in my work already. But the vibrancy of that realisation catapulted me into a new existence. I'd let go of the excess baggage I'd been carrying. I had forgiven myself, and I chose to forgive those who'd hurt me in the past. I asked for love, compassion and lightness. I decided to write my own set of principles on how I would live my life moving forward. I didn't need past conditioning to keep pulling me back into old ways, so with a clean sheet of paper, I wrote my guiding principles for my life.

I will suspend judgment of myself and others. I will see with fresh eyes. I will be receptive and open to explore and understand the entirety of a situation, rather than only listening from a place of past knowledge. I will see things from new angles, new perspectives, not just focus on what is familiar. I will listen with inquisitiveness about the possibilities that are available to me. I will value all of who I am, including my vulnerabilities and see this as a strength, not a weakness.

I will embrace my emotions, feel them and when required, sit with them. I will not push them down or hide how I feel. I will be kind to myself and will continue to give myself compassion, kindness, forgiveness, warmth, generosity, and gratitude. I will open my heart fully; I will embrace peace within. I will have self-ease, love for myself, and a deeper connection to the gratitude I have for myself and others. I will open myself up to the magic I have inside me. My light will shine bright, and I will trust my inner knowing. I will experience only the truth; I will pay attention to my intuition and allow this to guide me in everything I do. I will no longer force or push to achieve; I will allow true emergence to unfold. My intentions will come from my place of knowing, and I will no longer need to second guess, dumb down or hide who I am. I will accept my personal power and allow myself to be guided by my higher self.

A decade on, the business was thriving, and the profits increasing. I kept my feet on the ground. I knew materialistic things would not make me happy. I focused on what I currently had and appreciated what was already in my life. I was humble and felt lucky to have all this joy and success and, more than anything, doing work that was my vocation. The work I was doing was meaningful; it was helping others – I loved everything about the work I was involved in. The experiences I had reflected who I was, and they took me closer home to my true self.

I was using my gifts and talents creatively, and I was sharing them with others. I knew if I could work more in this way, it would bring deeper fulfilment and lifelong happiness. I felt it was part of my role to help others nurture their gifts and talents too. I was teaching this to our students, coaching people to connect with their natural gifts and talents, and I found more and more clients were asking me to help them find their purpose. I hadn't even articulated mine, and I was here helping them find theirs. The work was more than what I could have dreamed of. I felt privileged and honoured to be having these conversations with those I worked with. Helping others find their purpose would help me find mine. Finding my dharma was the final part of this journey.

I posed the questions, 'What is my purpose? What is my dharma? How can I use what I know, what I have, those things that are uniquely mine, and how can I let them shine more?' To do this, I brought in aspects of the previous steps we have taken. I first went back to my strengths and asked myself:

What's my story?

What am I good at?

When am I at my best?

What are the strengths others acknowledge in me?

I decided to tap into my core values.

What are my top 5 values?

What do I stand for?

What helps me make choices?

I reviewed and articulated my passions.

What do I love?

What excites me?

What am I drawn to?

Once I had all this down on a piece of paper, I could start to define my purpose. I had to create my purpose statement. I posed myself the question again, 'what is my purpose?' I decided to meditate on it so I could quieten my mind. When meditating, I had a vision of working as a teacher, sharing my knowledge and healing people through my words. I looked healthy, in fact, glowing. I was peaceful, and as I walked out into the sunshine, I moved with ease and grace.

Awaiting me in the sunshine was a group of women who were learning how to embrace themselves, reconnect and re-establish who they were. I was the teacher, and through my teachings, they were healing themselves. I could even see what I was wearing, but what struck me most about this vision was the feeling I had when I came out of my meditation practice, and that was one of coming home. It was as though I had arrived home. There was a sense of comfort, a place of knowing and although I couldn't place the location of where I was in my vision, it felt like I was home, home within me.

I continued to pose myself that question and the vision reappeared; sometimes, the groups changed in size, and the environment shifted. One time I was on stage addressing a huge audience of people, and other times it was more intimate in setting. Each time this vision came to me, I could feel something stir deep within. Each time the stirring got stronger and stronger, but I didn't know what to do with it.

I reminded myself that true joy comes from the very nature of who we are, and by tapping into myself, joy was always there within me to unfold and manifest in all aspects of my life. It felt that I was returning to wholeness; I was nearly home to my true self. The vision returned again. I didn't quite know how to make it happen but one wet Saturday afternoon, I sat at the kitchen table and announced out of the blue, 'I want to create something new; it's going to be called OneLife.' I doodled on the paper I'd brought with me. Within an hour, I had designed a range of new personal development programmes to support others to develop and grow as I had. Was this it – my purpose?

I reflected on my journey so far and accepted my life was a gift; the experiences I'd had were necessary. The trust in myself that I had developed over the years had continued to bring a lightness into my life; I knew it would lead me to where I needed to be. I embraced it. It was contagious, and I learned that I was resourceful and creative. I was a lifelong learner, and I loved putting my learning into practice. I lived and breathed it; I lit up when talking about it. I was energised and enthusiastic. I was fuelled by curiosity, and my creativity was driven by my desire to learn and experience more. So, I posed the questions again: 'What is my purpose? What is my dharma? How can I use what I know, what I have, those things that are uniquely mine, and how can I let them shine?'

This was not about having to do something extra; it was about simply showing up in my own life and sharing my uniqueness. I started to pay attention to what those I knew brought to a situation, a conversation or even the relationship. Everyone had something to offer another person. Everyone around me contributed to the welfare of another. I started to think about how other people benefited from my gifts and talents and how I could share mine more beyond what I was already doing. I needed to pull together all of what I had been learning over the years. I was a healer, a teacher, and a coach. In these moments, I went beyond self; it was not self-serving at all. The work I was doing was for them.

When I observed my friends in conversation, Fiona brought insightfulness to everything she did. Her talent for connecting others was something quite unique. The timing of those connections, the importance of those connections, was her gift. Irish Caroline spoke a truth that would send shivers down your spine. She had the ability to say what others wouldn't; her bravery in communicating something that needed to be addressed was her gift. She could cut right through the backstory and home in on something of great importance. Within seconds.

I decided to open myself up more. I started to share myself with others and did not expect anything back in return. I used what was unique to me and what came naturally to me. I didn't seek or wait for recognition. I didn't seek approval, acceptance or praise from other people. I did it with the intention to serve. I was learning to honour my whole self. I was the instrument, and I'd finally managed to fine-tune myself. The fog lifted, and I saw my dharma, my purpose. I was here to walk others back home to their true self.

In the process of walking myself home, I had discovered my life's purpose. That was why I had to experience what I did. This is why I'm here; this is what I'm meant to do. I let go of searching and embraced my new awareness. I could walk my path to freedom. I now knew where I was heading. I trusted myself, and I trusted the universe. I chose to allow my vision, the one that had visited me often, to become my reality. All I needed to do was to fully let go. To surrender to the universe and allow the unfolding of what was meant to be.

Exercise

So, now it's your turn to do the same. We can only do this when we have an open mind, open heart and open will. This statement will not be created in your mind; you need to connect with it deeply right in your core, but you also need to connect with the love in your heart for the life you will lead and share with others.

So, let's tune in, get centred and connected. Use your breathing exercises to create the space within you. Ego may present itself, but mindfully allow it to float away and just focus on what is real – your truth. There are no restrictions, only infinite possibilities.

What may help is to quieten the mind and do a short meditation and visualisation technique that will connect you in a deeper way. To do this, you can focus on your breathing, pay attention only to your breath, the inflow and outflow. Please don't force or control your breath; just allow the breath to naturally flow in and out of your body. With every inhale and exhale, you feel more relaxed; just breathe. Now move your awareness to your heart centre, feel the warmth and connection to the love you have for yourself. Stay here for a moment longer, keep breathing and let the warmth wash over you.

Now, as you breathe, I want you to expand your connection to all, inhale, make the connection beyond self, allow your energy, your love, and compassion to extend and expand, let it flow freely – you may feel you have grown a little taller as your energy expands, but you shouldn't expect to feel any different apart from a greater sense of connection. Keep breathing and let the sensation you have flow from you. Stay in this place, remain connected and just breathe from this space of being.

Ask yourself the following questions and connect with the answers that appear. Feel them, know them and be them.

- Who am I?
- Who do I see?
- What do I hear?
- What do I feel?
- Who am I?

Keep breathing and stay connected to how you feel and who you are.

- What do I want?
- What am I doing?
- Where am I?
- How do I feel?
- What do I want?

Keep breathing and stay connected to how you feel and what you want.

- What is my purpose?
- What am I meant to be?
- What am I here to do?
- How can I serve?
- What is my purpose?

Keep breathing and stay connected to your purpose.

Now write your purpose statement.

Remember to envision the impact you'll have on your world as a result of living your purpose. Your actions – not your words – are what really matter.

My purpose is...

Once you have written down your purpose, remember you are not expected to do anything else with it just now, apart from letting your purpose statement resonate and settle. Keep saying it daily and allow yourself to fully connect with it.

As Oprah Winfrey says, 'Start embracing the life that is calling you. Find your calling, know what sparks light in you so you – in your own way – can illuminate the world.'

8

CHAPTER 12

Coming Home

'There is no place like home.'

L. Frank Baum

I've always loved watching the film *The Wizard of Oz*. There is something so familiar about Dorothy clicking her red shoes and saying, 'There is no place like home.'

We are here on our last step, our arrival, back home to our true selves. It is important we consolidate what we have learned so far and also lock in the final piece of the jigsaw. In this final chapter, we will complete this part of our journey together. This is not the end; in fact, it is just the beginning.

You will continue to move forward on your own journey. It is important we sustain and maintain what we have learned so far. But equally important is your openness and readiness for what comes next.

Let's just take a minute to reflect on the lessons learned so far.

We started with learning how to quieten the mind, and you should now be able to practise meditation regularly or even daily, and I am sure you are seeing the benefits of regular practice. You will have a clear understanding of who you are based upon the mirror work we did in Chapter 2, followed by learning how to be true to yourself. You now know what's a perception versus your reality and have explored those self-limiting beliefs you had. In Chapter 6, we learned how to let go to let come and focused on having an open mind, open heart and open will. Without looking inwards, we would never have been able to reach where we are today.

We have explored your passions and how we can incorporate experiential living into our lives. Being in the moment whilst also using your own unique gifts and talents and sharing those with others. This was quickly followed by understanding the purpose of self-care and the need to regularly top up your tank; all of these lessons that you've learned to master have finally led us to where we are now. Your purpose has been defined, and your arrival home to your true self is imminent.

The final step is to create your 'on purpose affirmation.' This is where you ground and anchor your purpose so we can create and implement your strategy for living your life with purpose, passion and in your greatest potential – as your true self.

Doing this can be described as part celebration and acknowledgement of all the things you have achieved and learned so far, and the second part is figuring out how you are going to remain home and live your life on purpose.

Let me explain what I mean by an on purpose affirmation. For me an affirmation is a statement that has meaning, is significant to you, and it sets your inner compass to your true self and your consciousness. It is a personal statement aligned to your core being, written as though it has already happened.

When you say it out loud, you are reflecting on your story as though it has already happened. This is described as the law of attraction, and many have described this as the most powerful law of the universe. It is the law that determines the complete order of the universe. Every moment of your life and everything you experience in your life. Simply put, the law of attraction is the ability to attract into our lives what we want. It is believed regardless of age, nationality, or religious belief, we are all susceptible to the laws that govern the universe, unlocking the law of attraction. The law of attraction uses the power of the mind to translate what we want into a reality. Like attracts like, and we can manifest our dreams, aspirations and goals.

This is similar to Deepak Chopra's description of the law of intention and desire in *The Seven Spiritual Laws of Success.* He says that 'the field of pure potentiality is influenced by intention and desire.' Basically, what we are doing with an affirmation is calling forth what we want so the universe can help this manifest. By calling forth what you want through your affirmation, through your thoughts, feelings and desires means that two influences will be activated in your consciousness. Attention and Intention. Attention enlivens, and intention transforms.

So, where does this all come from?

The practices and beliefs in the law of attraction have been igniting the lives of great individuals throughout the course of history.

Over the years, this evolved, and the concept spread into western culture and became the term karma. Based also on the work of quantum physicists proves that the power of the mind has an incredible impact on what we can manifest. The basic principle is what you give out to the world is ultimately what you get back in return – that is why we have needed to do the work we have done so far to arrive at this point.

We are the creators and controllers of our life, and we can shape our life and the world around us. Once we accept the possibilities that life has to offer us, we come to realise that, like an artist, we can create pictures of our intended life. We can then make choices and take actions that will realise what we have envisaged. The beauty of this is, if we don't like the picture we have painted, we can change it. Life is a blank canvas of possibility; you can always paint another picture. Life is not set in stone, nothing is permanent, and if we give ourselves permission to believe this, then your life will keep evolving, you will keep growing, and your experiences will be infinite. Hence, your journey is not over; it is just beginning.

To come home fully to your true self, you will need to master your attention and intention by creating your on purpose affirmation. According to the law of attraction, what you think and feel shapes your reality. It's like what we said before in one of our earlier chapters, what you think you believe, what you believe you become. Therefore, the power of affirmations lies in the ability to transform your external world by first changing your internal one. We have spent a lot of time doing the inner work required to come home, and now we need to turn our attention to sharing our intention with the universe. By drawing attention to how we want to be living our lives, we can then set our intention on how that will manifest.

To make the affirmation work, you need to write down what will happen in the future *as if it had already happened*. When you finalise your on purpose affirmation, you are required to understand the four golden rules that need to be followed in line with the law of attraction.

The Golden Rules

1. Write your affirmation down

2. Say it out loud so the universe can hear it

3. Believe it will happen – pay attention to your intention

4. Show gratitude when your affirmation starts to become a reality

When writing your affirmation, you should not limit yourself in any way or even think about how you are going to get there; all you need to focus on is what you have achieved, what you've accomplished and how you feel about what's happened. However, the one thing you do need to do is make sure that your affirmation is meaningful, significant and your desires are connected to living your life on purpose, with passion and in your potential.

Your affirmation should start with:

My name is [add in your full name]. It's [add in the month and year – exactly 12 months to the day, in the future]. I've had an amazing year, and these are the reasons why.

It is at this point that you write down everything that will happen from now until then – as though it had already happened. Please take your time to write this down, remembering your words should come from your place of knowing, not from your head. Do not judge, analyse or limit yourself in any way.

That is Step 1. Once you have your on purpose affirmation, you now need to read it and say it out loud so the universe can hear your desire. It may feel strange to read it out to an open space, but this is a very important step in the law of attraction. That is Step 2.

Step 3 is about believing it and paying attention to your intentions. So, like your purpose statement, it is important that you revisit your on purpose affirmation as this is what will keep your attention focused so it will enliven your intention, which will then, over time, transform into your reality. Your on purpose affirmation will become your life, your way of being.

Finally, Step 4 is about showing gratitude as and when your affirmation starts to come true. So, when things happen, all you need to do is acknowledge them and show gratitude. Showing gratitude will keep you fully grounded and centred; it will also keep you humble. This is crucial to the success of you living your purpose. Ego, as we know, will always reside within us, but we can manage it as long as we stay grounded and humble regardless of the success we have. Humility is the key to your success.

I wrote my affirmation – I chose not to go too far into the future but enough to set my inner compass. I decided that I would revisit this exercise each year as I wanted to fully surrender to what would unfold. I knew that being too prescriptive, such as ten years from now, would potentially limit me, so I chose 12 months ahead. I let go, and I invited the universe to guide me.

My name is Gillian McMichael; it's December 2022, and I've had an amazing year, and these are the reasons why. My book *Coming Home* was published; I felt so proud of what I had written and shared. It was a true representation of how I used all my 20 years of experience to help me come back home to myself, and I know it will help others do the same. I have just completed the fourth season of the Full Circle Podcast, *Finding your way home*, and I have been so privileged to meet and interview some amazing people. Every time I hear a guest's story, I am humbled by their courage and determination to overcome their obstacles.

These experiences – the book and the podcast – have allowed me to really show up in my own life, both personally and professionally. The programmes I have delivered this year have been much deeper and more fulfilling. I am teaching and coaching at a deeper level, and I feel those I work with are having greater transformational shifts than ever before. The business is going well, and work from new and current clients is pouring in. My meditation practice has deepened, and I am loving the life routine I crafted. My exercise is consistent, and so is my diet. I have maintained a good, healthy life routine, and I am outside in nature. Which I love. As a family, we have remained connected, and our relationships have also deepened. I managed the transition well when my son moved to university, and I am a very proud mum. Ross and I are loving spending time with each other, and we have spent quality time with our friends and wider family.

As I enter my 50th year, I feel and look great. I am confident, and I feel peace within. I have shown up every day as my true self, and I am grounded, resourceful, creative and whole. I have reached more of my potential, and I know there is so much there for me to tap into. I am very grateful for the life I have created, and I will continue to nurture what I have and what is also to come.

I feel loved, and I give love readily to those in my life. I have kept my promises to myself all the way through 2022. Be kind to myself, be honest with myself, believe in myself and trust myself. These have served me well, and by living by them, I am on track. I am still home; I am aligned, and I am walking my true path. Thank you, and I am excited about the year ahead.

It is important to frequently read your affirmation out loud and do this at least once a month, but you could revisit it more. As I reflected on my journey over the last decade, I remembered one of my Vedic meditation teachers saying, 'Life should flow like the flow of a sacred river, surrender fully to your sense of knowing in that moment, be courageous and bold. Let go of any struggle and surrender back to the flow of the river, and you will regain your harmony. It's at these moments when we need to be fully conscious and pay attention to those feelings of our inner guide, the voice that reminds us we are not in flow.'

8

Completion

'Love is the bridge between you and everything.'

Rumi

'May today there be peace within. May you trust you are exactly where you are meant to be. May you not forget the infinite possibilities that are of faith in yourself and others. May you use the gifts that you have received and pass on the love that had been given to you. May you be content with yourself just the way you are. Let this knowledge settle into your bones and allow your soul the freedom to sing, dance, praise and love. It is there for each and every one of us.' – Mother Teresa

Your life should reflect the gentle flow of the sacred river. You have the personal power to surrender to the flow of life. You have the choice to swim upstream or let go and allow the universe to guide you. Everything you need is already there, inside you. Do nothing more than honour your true self. You have a well of wisdom within you. You have a deep sense of knowing. A golden thread that will keep you aligned and connected to your true self.

There will be times beyond now where you will wobble. You will momentarily disconnect and lose your alignment. All you have to do is remember, take a pause for breath, give yourself compassion and the gift of forgiveness. Accept in these moments there is a lesson for you to learn. Embrace it, don't fight it, and when ready, reverse back into yourself and reconnect.

It is your gift. It is your life. Love you for being you. Let yourself be seen. Show up as you and only you. You are home, and there is no place quite like it.

References

Stephen B. Karpman, *A Game Free Life*, Drama Triangle
Publications, 2014

Otto Scharmer, *Theory U*, Berrett-Koehler Publishers, 2007

Deepak Chopra, *The Seven Spiritual Laws of Success*,
Bantam Press, 1993

The Author

 Gillian McMichael is a Master Transformational Coach, Chopra Centre Meditation, Ayurveda, Perfect Health Teacher and Reiki Energy Healer. She has also been a coach training educator, a coach mentor and coach supervisor for 20 years.

Gillian has supported over 10,000 clients overcome their barriers to success. Moving beyond fear to elicit agency in those she works with. Gillian walks her clients back home to their true selves. She embodies a holistic, whole-person approach and has become one of the leading voices in transformational coaching and development.

Gillian has been transforming lives for over two decades, and through these intimate conversations with highly functioning and performing people, she realised her life story reflects many of the themes she saw in her clients. This work is the capstone of her career in the service of transforming – she has created a formula through her life story to help and serve others.

Gillian is the host of her Full Circle Podcast, *Finding your way home*. She is a keynote speaker and delivers global transformational retreats and workshops. This is her first book and one she felt compelled to write.

www.fullcircleglobal.com

@the.master.coach

https://www.linkedin.com/in/gillian-mcmichael